STRESS-FREE MARRIAGE

STRESS-FREE MARRIAGE

*Does your marriage produce
or prevent stress?*

Dave and Joyce Ames

Foreword by
Larry Crabb

CROSSWAY BOOKS
Eastbourne

First edition 1991 published by Crossway Books, Eastbourne, E. Sussex.

ISBN 1 85684 008 5

Production and Printing in England for
C R O S S W A Y   B O O K S
Glyndley Manor, Pevensey, Eastbourne, East Sussex BN24 5BS by
Nuprint Ltd, Station Road, Harpenden, Herts AL5 4SE.

Contents

Preface

The most important reason for reading this preface is to understand why a book by two people is written in the first person. When two people write together they either agree to write certain sections, or one finds the actual wording subject to the other's agreement. We use the latter: I write and Joyce criticises, as we sometimes say. Regardless of who finds the majority of the words, the book is still very much a team effort. The author is the one with the ideas, not the one who does the typing. In our last two books we used a neutral voice, except when one of us wanted to be a bit more personal. Then we would have to say something like I (Dave) or I (Joyce) before we could make a first person statement. I found that unwieldy. I wanted to be fairly vulnerable in this book and the most effective way to accomplish that is to write the entire book—I (Dave). When I talk about what 'we' did or 'our' opinion, I am referring to us as a husband and wife team.

My interest in stress began during my career in medical administration. I had special training in psychology, preventative medicine, aerospace medicine and aircraft accident investigation, all of which deal with stress. I suppose it was my familiarity of the subject going back to the 1950s that made me view the current preoccupation with it like the wheel had been reinvented. For some reason I never thought too much about it from a biblical perspective. In 1980 a consultant friend of mine put together a series of talks on the subject and showed me his notes. I responded politely, but I'm afraid it appeared to me to be yet another attempt to proof-text a psychological theory.

It wasn't until we met Dr Bill Munro and his wife Francis, who conduct seminars on stress, that we took notice. Bill was dealing with stress as a medical officer for the Post Office, but he could see that the Bible had the answers the world was missing. We asked them what sort of things they taught on their courses that couldn't be taught at the Post Office. Their answer was 'Oh we talk about things like forgiveness, the real meaning of love, a biblical self-image, just the basic biblical principles that seemed to elude the average Christian.'

These were the very things we had been hammering away at for years in our seminars and residential marriage weekends. Certainly the majority of the couples who came to us for counselling were experiencing stress as the direct result of failing to apply those principles.

The idea of a book on stress in marriage was a refreshing concept because it allows us to write a book on marriage that doesn't have to tell everything a couple ought to know on the subject. This book focuses in on the most common pressure points in marriage and this allows special treatment without making it a massive volume.

Dave for Dave and Joyce Ames
20 Mill Street, Mildenhall, Suffolk IP28 7DP

Acknowledgements

We owe a great deal to our good friend Vina Green, a graduate level English teacher, who spent a lot of time poring over this manuscript to assure our thoughts were effectively communicated.

When I was in school I didn't appreciate receiving papers back covered with red marks. I felt intimidated by questions in the margins such as 'What is the antecedent to this pronoun?' I still think English teachers can be very deflating, slashing away with their red sabres. I was living under the illusion that I had improved since my school days. Her ministry to us did make me think of how some people might feel reading this book recognising the need to change.

Dedication

Gordon Westbrook graduated, with honours, from this lifetime character development course, in which every believer is enrolled, on 12 December 1990. We would like to offer this book as a small memorial to the high regard in which he was held by all who knew him. He was light years ahead of most of us in demonstrating the gentleness and respect so crucial to the type of love we are called to. He was also the chairman of Mission to Marriage.

Foreword

by

Dr Larry Crabb

Not many Christian leaders manage to combine a tender and perceptive awareness of human need with an uncompromising commitment to the immediate relevance of biblical truth. Too often, folks respond with compassion to personal hurt, but offer help that has little to do with the central truths of Christianity. Others can seem 'pompously biblical' and, as they proclaim the truth, miss the real pain people live with every day.

In this excellent book, Dave and Joyce Ames reflect a knowledgeable confidence in the Bible that strengthens their ability to speak directly and sensitively to couples in stress. The well written chapters are liberally sprinkled with rich thoughts worthy of serious reflection such as 'Self-preservation becomes a relationship problem when we allow our fear of being hurt to get in the way of our ability to love' (p. 84). No simplistic formulas here, just careful discussion of God's perspective on the things we find so puzzling and distressing.

The authors build all their ideas on a solidly biblical foundation. They clearly know what real life is like because they live honestly with themselves and speak meaningfully with scores of people God sends their way. And they write with warmth and compassion. I am therefore pleased to recommend this book and their ministry as especially valuable in the vital work of providing married couples (and others) with truly biblical help.

Tyndale House
Cambridge
England

Introduction

THE 'IDEAL' MARRIAGE

Lord Jacobovits, while Britain's chief rabbi, claimed the Jews considered the home as a personal temple which made it a sacred place of sanctuary. He attributed their surviving millenniums of persecution to this sanctifying of their homes which allowed them to regenerate the necessary strength to go back out and face yet again more persecution.

A home that is a refuge of regeneration provides the opportunity to deal with the pressures of life and thereby prevent stress.

Conversely, I think it is fair to say that any family where the members fail to appreciate their responsibility to minister to the needs of their fellow members will, to some degree, create pressure. It would be an overstatement to say all families that produce pressure are the result of marriages that produce pressure, but it is generally the case.

Marriage, by its very definition, is the most secure of all human relationships. As marriage partners, we are meant to have the security of knowing there is one other human being who will never abandon us. We should also expect to be strengthened, encouraged and challenged by our partners. There is one other person who will always be at our side—who will share the journey with us. When all others turn their backs on us or let us down, we have the confidence that our partner will continue to support us.

When the world is slinging mud at us we know our partner will be out there with soap and a scrubbing brush to clean us off.

We know that this is a valid description, if for no other reason than the fact that God has deliberately used marriage as an illustration of the relationship of Christ to his church. And Christ said he would never abandon his bride, the church. He would always be by her side strengthening and comforting her and would present her without spot or wrinkle.

It would be easy to label the above description as ideal. We know that this concept is far different from what many couples experience. There are, after all, nearly half as many partners abandoning each other every year as there are couples getting married. And the majority of those who do stay together are not experiencing anything like the security described.

It is the very lack of this security which for many is a major contributing factor to the stress in their lives.

The fact that this description is considered ideal may be precisely where the problem lies. Having a partner who is committed to our well-being is the intended characteristic of a marriage and not just an ideal. It is a poor choice of terms to use 'ideal' for a quality which is actually intended.

According to noted author, David Pawson: 'To introduce the unbiblical, Platonic notion of an "ideal" [is a] fatal flaw. The dictionary defines this as impracticable; its synonym is "romantic". In ordinary speech it signifies an unattainable standard relevant only to an "ideal" world. The Sermon on the Mount has been dismissed as "idealistic".'[1]

It may be that a major cause of impotent Christian lives among those committed believers who claim to hold God's word in high regard is the fact that they have labelled too much of his plan *Ideal*.

When marriage partners function in faith that there is one person who will always be at their side to share the journey, to strengthen, encourage, and challenge them, they find their marriage to be an effective bastion against the pressures of life. Those who consider it idealistic frequently find their marriage a source of pressure rather than a defence against it.

Another fact observed over years of counselling Christian couples is this:

When one partner sees marital security as something attainable and fully assumes his or her responsibility, regardless of what the other is doing, they create a special 'canopy of grace' which makes it easier for their partner to fulfil their responsibility.

This canopy simply creates an environment more conducive to functioning as one should. We all know it's easier to be nice to nice people, so why not make it easier for our partner. Waiting until they deserve it is not the way to show love. It is certainly not what God intended.

Unfortunately many of us are extremely sceptical; we have been hurt and let down and we don't think it wise to go all-out in a relationship until we are sure that the other person is assuming their share of the responsibility. After all, we become pretty vulnerable when we *'submit to one another out of reverence for Christ'* as Paul admonishes in Ephesians. When a marriage partner functions with a cautious wait-and-see attitude this brings pressure on the other partner. Someone has to break the cycle of self-preservation with vulnerable love.

God never intended us to take some leap-in-the-dark step of faith, to place all our trust in a marriage partner who also has feet of clay. He intended us to trust in him and his sovereign plan.

The secret to a marriage which stands against pressure, rather than creating it, is not finding the perfect partner. It is following God's plan designed to make us more perfect partners.

Most of the time we have three to five current files on couples who are coming to see us because their marriage is under pressure and they are suffering stress. We don't spend much time on popular theories for *coping* with stress, because our goal is not to learn to live with stress but to eliminate it. God's plan for life is also a plan for *eliminating* or *preventing* stress. Stress is fairly insidious and can often become firmly established before we recognise it.

The fact that we teach a type of marital stress prevention doesn't mean we never find ourselves in a state of stress. This happened to Joyce approximately two years following our son's death. As she tells it:

> I was feeling great, physically, emotionally, spiritually. We were working fairly hard at the time, but I was certainly at peace with myself and the world.
>
> Then one Thursday afternoon our secretary's twelve year old son was hit by a car while riding his bicycle. He died two days later. We felt well qualified to empathise with Linda and Colin and became as involved as possible. We took in meals, housed the relatives that came over from Ireland, and even hosted the get together after the funeral.
>
> I grieved for Linda and Colin as they faced their loss, but I also was aware that my grieving was deeper. I was grieving all over again for our son Bill who had been killed in a motor accident two years before. At this time I was swimming every morning, but I developed some breathing problems. Going up and down stairs tired me and I developed some chest pains. I stopped the swimming and slowed down, but my physical condition worsened. I began over indulging in sweets. It took a few weeks for me to wake up to the fact that my physical problems were the result of grieving again for Bill.
>
> I finally had a day alone with God in our back garden pouring my heart out to him and getting his grace for my situation. The eating came back under control and I was at peace, but I still tired easily.
>
> I remember asking God a few days later why I was still tired and what I should do about it. 'Rest' was the word that came to my mind but I had difficulty believing that was from God considering there was so much to do.
>
> Weeks went by, but the shortness of breath stayed with me and I finally went to the doctor who ran some tests. Of course, the first thing he asked me was, 'How are things at home?' I knew what he was after. If I told him the circum-

stances at the onset of this problem, he would assume it was stress and look no farther. But I knew these symptoms could fit dozens of purely physical problems. It was nothing spiritual or psychological. I had prayed my problem through in the garden. I knew how to handle stress; after all we were writing a book about it.

I went back to the doctor three more times for tests. They could find nothing and each time he would ask the same question. By now I was not only breathless and tired, but my mind seemed to have slowed down and I couldn't remember things. We were at a conference when it all reached a climax. One of our colleagues at the conference is a neurologist and Dave suggested I chat with him, that he might shed some light on it. We both secretly suspected a brain tumour. A neurologist can rule out a lot of major problems, including a high percentage of brain tumours, with no more sophisticated equipment than a pen light and a pin. He, of course, found no physical reason for my symptoms either but because he was a friend I began telling him the whole story.

A strange thing happened as I began to share with him about the death of Linda's son and my grieving over Bill. I started crying again and conviction came to me that I really was experiencing stress. My body was reacting to the emotional strain it had been under. When I had asked God what to do about the breathlessness, the word 'rest' I had heard really was God's answer. That was what my body needed at that time.

Once I admitted being in a state of stress and realised my need to rest, I was all right. The physical symptoms cleared almost immediately. The Lord just didn't want me lying to myself about where I was. I never felt any condemnation from him, only understanding and comfort. I became acutely aware that when God allows pressure he is always there with his grace, even if we wait until we're stressed before accepting it.

We often refer to the Bible as *The Manufacturer's Instruction Manual* and this is particularly germane to the problem of stress. Any piece of equipment we purchase which comes with an instruction manual does so because it is possible to misuse it, generally making it less efficient and often damaging the equipment. Life comes with an instruction manual because it is possible to misuse it, generally making it less efficient and often damaging the equipment.

This is not a modern notion. Jesus' parable in Matthew 7:24-27 is exactly the same concept.

> Therefore everyone who hears these words of mine and puts them into practice is like a wise man who built his house on the rock. The rain came down, the streams rose, and the winds blew and beat against that house; yet it did not fall, because it had its foundation on the rock. But everyone who hears these words of mine and does not put them into practice is like a foolish man who built his house on sand. The rain came down, the streams rose, and the winds blew and beat against that house, and it fell with a great crash.

No individual or married couple is exempt from the storms of life. The couples who will stand through the pressure of the storm are not the couples who simply read *The Manufacturer's Instruction Manual*.

It won't be the couples who hear the word of God, or even those who are conversant with it who will withstand the pressures of life. It will be the couples who put God's word into practice.

Actually living out the principles of love, forgiveness, servanthood, acceptance etc, with one another is the rock that causes us to withstand those outside forces that beat against us.

We will be examining this topic in three distinct parts.

Part One Examining the Problem looks at several stressful marriage situations. It defines stress and makes several helpful distinctions between pressure and stress.

Part Two God's Basic Stress Prevention examines four extremely significant pillars of our faith and their direct

influence on stress. It also shows how these truths have
been distorted and the toll this has taken on true objective
love.

Part Three God's Specific Stress Prevention for Marriage
demonstrates the practical application of these basic truths
in every day married life.

NOTE

1. David Pawson: From a letter to the Editor of *Leadership Today*
on the controversy over Homosexuals among Church of England
Clergy 1987.

Part One

EXAMINING THE PROBLEM

1

Marriages Under Pressure

THE AFFAIR

Brian and Dorothy were discreetly referred to us as an emergency case. Dorothy had just confessed to her husband that she had had an affair with her employer. Brian was eager to mend the situation and felt it would be wise to seek help. Their church was without a pastor so a friend directed them to us.

These were fairly early days for us, but even then we knew that the primary cause of unfaithfulness among women is husbands who don't seem to appreciate them. (Nothing ever justifies adultery but it can be guarded against.) Brian and Dorothy were an attractive couple and each claimed the other was a good marriage partner. Brian came across as much more practical than romantic, but that's not the unpardonable sin. They were approaching their silver wedding anniversary and had two grown children. They described their relationship as very normal, but they also told us that Dorothy had been involved in another affair ten years before.

We were able to do a fair amount which was useful in helping the couple toward the healing they were so desperately seeking. We explored several avenues, such as bitterness in the innocent party which so frequently accompanies adultery, but nothing led us to feel we were actually dealing with the root cause of the problem. Then they invited us to come to their home for one of the sessions, which proved to be very enlightening.

They showed us around the house pointing out modifications and additions which Brian had very skilfully completed. When we went out into the garden to view Dorothy's efforts Brian seemed to be manoeuvering us around to a large shed at the back of his garage. He opened the door with a flair and *voila!* there it was, the root problem, or at least the physical manifestation of it.

The shed not only contained a very business like workshop boasting a metal turning lathe, it also contained a 1934 MG roadster in better condition than many cars come from the factory. Owning a 1934 MG roadster does not in itself place pressure on a marriage, but the way that this one went from an initial investment of £200 to approximately £20,000 was not all inflation. Brian was an extremely skilled amateur engineer who was able to make any part that he could not purchase.

He had spent thousands of hours tenderly restoring this piece of motoring history to its present glory. It places a woman under a fair amount of pressure being faithful to a man who is having an affair with a 1934 MG roadster. However, ignoring one's partner is not the only thing which brings pressure into a marriage.

BIG BUSINESS—SMALL PROFIT

Don and Sharon, whom we have known for several years now, are a husband/wife team who make their living as marketing consultants to major corporations. Don is an extremely bright visionary. Sharon, when not working on a project for their own company, has no problem finding other companies who would like her to join one of their projects at a daily fee larger than many a weekly salary.

Unfortunately, all of Don's visions have not led to immediate financial reward. Their own consultation service hasn't actually entered into orbit yet, and they have only kept it aloft with the money they have earned working for other companies. They have been loaned money at several points in their career by family and friends but have been able to pay back only token amounts.

They have their differences: he is basically a conservative evangelical and she tends much more to be charismatic. This has caused some consternation. But this pales into oblivion next to their differences over finances. Managing large sums of money in business and dealing effectively with one's own finances can frequently be two separate issues. Don correctly sees success in business as directly related to the service he is able to provide. However, he sees his opportunity to provide that service as directly related to his image. In general, this involves first rate clothes, cars and clubs.

Not long ago we received a panic phone call from Sharon asking if she could please come and spend some time with us. It seemed that Don had bought a Porsche (for the company), a new stereo, membership in a very up-market health club, a time share in Madeira and was now negotiating for an apartment in central London so he wouldn't have to drive home when he wanted to work overtime.

Sharon told us when she arrived that she was paying the mortgage on their home in the commuter belt as well as the routine outgoings. Don's bills were one and a half times his income and he wanted her to pick up the slack. None of these recent purchases were the result of a joint decision. The time share and the new flat were the only ones she had even an inkling of in advance and she had specifically registered her failure to understand how they could possibly afford them.

By this time Don had been suffering tension headaches for some time and Sharon was developing an intestinal complaint which her physician thought to be stress induced.

It soon became evident that it wasn't the hard work propping up a failing business, nor the financial bondage in and of itself which was pushing this marriage to the brink of disaster. These are all high pressure issues in themselves. The thing Sharon found hardest to bear was the unilateral decisions. Most people can stand a good deal of hard work

and even the embarrassment that many associate with out-
standing debts, as long as they feel they are a respected part
of the team. Wives are no exception. Making decisions
which involve another person's life, without consulting
them, in no way conveys the message that they are
respected—just the opposite, it communicates disrespect.
Disrespect and its close relative, rejection, probably introduce more pressure per square inch of marriage than any
other issue.

THE OTHER WOMAN

Doreen came forward at a Billy Graham crusade. In addition to a new life in Christ she told her counsellor that she
needed help with her marriage. She knew that her husband,
Rob, had come forward the night before and was full of the
joy of the Lord. They were referred to us and came for a
visit a week later. Their presentation problem was twofold
according to Doreen. She wrote: 'I cannot forgive my husband for having an affair.' Secondly they both stated that
their sex life was almost non-existent. It did not take too
much probing to conclude that the second problem was a
stress symptom of the first, even though they certainly
didn't recognise it.

They told us they had an appointment with a sex therapist in three months' time. We told them that they might as
well cancel it because if they couldn't work through the
forgiveness issue no sex therapist could enhance their love
life, and if they were successful with that, the sex problem
would disappear. It was a brash sounding statement, but
proved to be true.

For many marriages the most sensitive barometer of
their relationship is their sex life. If there is pressure in the
marriage it will frequently show itself here first. There is a
very good reason for this: sexual problems are 99% problems of the mind. Relationships consist of attitudes which
are also a matter of the mind. Therefore it is easy to
understand why sexual difficulties are quite frequently a

subconscious response to pressure generated in the marriage.

'AND THEY LIVED HAPPILY EVER AFTER'

Unfortunately, they don't all live happily ever after. Many end up in divorce courts. Others learn to live with stress because to them it seems easier than following God's plan. After all, wouldn't following God's plan cause some changes? Mightn't this require the yielding of one's rights, granting forgiveness, devotion to one's partner and maintaining a clear conscience, just to mention a few things? Of course it does. In fact it is not only the big glaring problems which require applied godliness, but also the day-in and day-out problems which require our adherence to the Maker's Manual to avoid them becoming major problems.

A year or so ago we were preparing to conduct a church-based marriage seminar when, on the day we were to depart, we received a letter from the pastor with another letter enclosed. He said he didn't know if the enclosed would be of any use to us but he was forwarding it out of respect to the deacon's wife who penned it. It read as follows:

Dear Jonathan.

I expect the Ames' have their talk already prepared but these are a few of the heartaches that have been shared and prayed about during the past year.
1. Our two year old is still sleeping in our bedroom. My husband does not do anything in the house and the back bedroom is full of junk! What can I do?
2. I am dreading my husband retiring. He just goes to work, comes home and watches TV. Doesn't have any hobbies or friends. How can I have him around all the time?
3. My wife expects me to start doing the cleaning and washing etc. when I come home after work. I don't mind helping, but feel she leaves it all for me. Please help.

4. We have sex every night. My husband won't take no even when I am unwell. I say sex not love making for that is what it has become, just the same old act. I do love him and would value some helpful instruction.

5. My husband will not pray or read the Bible with me. I have suggested it from time to time, but he will go and pray with others. I really would love to share this time and grow together.

6. My husband is sometimes moody and I get fed up with having to humour and be especially nice to him to bring him back to normality. Is this attitude right?

7. I guess we got married too young. Now I have the baby I am at home every day and all my husband does is go out anywhere and everywhere in the evenings, leaving me alone at night too. Football every Saturday. Oh dear, help please.

Yours in Him

Mary Wright

All of these are common problems that represent the warp and weft of every day married life. They all have several things in common. The first is the fact that either the stated problem or the handling of it violates God's plan. Each of the problems is placing pressure on the marriage. Any of these situations should be examined with the thought in mind that they may be the flashing red light on the instrument panel warning of a faulty commitment to please the Lord.

2

Christians Also Hurt

Many churches seem to promote the concept that Christians should always appear as though they were advertising tooth paste and function as though they were selling vitamins. The notion that because we are a new creation, we should have none of the old problems has caused many simply to bury the problems. This provides the catalyst for stress and undermines the foundation of many marriages.

Years ago a church we belonged to was going through the 'seated-in-the-heavenlies' stage. I ran into my pastor in a supermarket who asked 'How are you doing?' In my subjective opinion I wasn't doing very well. My oldest son had just written home for a large sum of money he needed in pursuit of his degree. The younger two were going through difficult places and I had just missed a big promotion at the office.

So I made the nearly fatal mistake of replying, 'Pretty good, under the circumstances.' That was not the 'institutional' answer. That wasn't where we were as a church. I had just failed the course. I also felt as though I had just walked into the jaws of some sort of Christian barracuda when he snapped back 'What do you mean, "under the circumstances"? Don't you know you are supposed to be on top of the circumstances? Don't you know we are seated in the heavenlies?' Fortunately, our marriage was at such a point that it provided all the human support I required, and it was a good thing.

This reply didn't come from one who always spoke in clichés. Our pastor didn't live in an ivory tower, nor did he make a practice of 'slaying people in the Spirit' or lengthening legs in a side show fashion. He was simply a well meaning pastor who understood the propensity of the human race to become mired in self-fulfilling prophecies of gloom and doom. He knew that concentration on the half truths we see before us can undercut our ability to appropriate the very real spiritual truths that we can only 'see through a glass darkly'. In other words, he wanted to lead me from a problem orientated mind-set to a focus that was solution orientated.

Unfortunately, he failed to understand a basic principle, along with a good deal of the Christian world.

People are difficult to lead on to a solution if they aren't convinced you understand the problem.

Most of us are not open to an objective assessment of our problem until we are convinced there is full appreciation of its subjective dimension. Empathy is a subjective word; it has to do with understanding people's feelings.

There are certain hyperactive Christians who seem to function with a mass marketing mentality, dispensing remedies which are about as personalised as junk mail. Surely they must be aware that their answer doesn't fit every problem but assume that by telling enough people they will eventually score. Will they receive a commission if it works? They surely give that impression. Meanwhile it does have its effect—the advice is rejected. The shame is that we have now become vaccinated against what may be the truth, simply because the truth was presented with a one-size-fits-all mentality.

Didn't Jesus say 'In this world you will have trouble'? Then why is it that those of us honest enough to admit we are experiencing trouble, pressure or difficulty are treated as spiritual adolescents? What about the Hebrews 11 'Honours List of Faith'? Were they jubilant at having not seen those things that were promised even at their death? It is hard to envisage a precedent for mirth in the face of adversity pondering that list of torturing, floggings, and imprisonment. It is especially difficult to understand someone being able to keep on smiling while being sawn in two.

Certainly I recognise that our modern day trials are in an entirely different league from the early church. Admittedly, the only shedding of blood I have suffered in the name of the kingdom has been paper cuts from folding prayer letters. However, there are times when I think shedding blood might be preferred by some who find themselves under extreme psychological pressure because of their stand. I can think of one plumber who spent a good deal of his last few years of employment in 'verbal isolation'. His 'sin' was to record accurately the amount of time he took to do a given job and the same for his travel time. This meant that his colleagues were forced to follow suit, lest their heavily padded time cards come into question. Naturally they bitterly resented this because it forced them into an honest day's work. He was fortunate in knowing that he had the support of his wife and daughter as he took this stand.

This is only one version of western societies' state-of-the-art martyrdom, but similar pressures are repeated thousands of times over. We could fill several chapters with the price that is being paid to be God's man or God's woman in the secular world. And every one of those men and women has times when they definitely feel 'under the circumstances'. But how many of them can talk about their loneliness or the fact that they are scared stiff—of reprisals, of losing their job, or demolishing their careers?

How many others are under the pressure of a guilty conscience due to failure to take a stand? A young aircraft mechanic once revealed to us that he was being forced to sign off certain checks that he was specifically told not to accomplish. His supervisor was overriding the maintenance procedures, sacrificing certain procedures which he was sure were actually redundant. He was doing so because his team could not possibly reach their quota if each member actually checked everything on the list. This young man was under pressure because he failed to take a stand. How many Christians do you know that you could share your failures with—especially when you know good and well the failure boils down to failure to obey God?

In times past when I had experienced a fairly depressing day, Joyce would ask how my day had gone, and my reply was frequently, 'Lions 6—Christian 0.' The lions, of course, were all those 'infidels' that God in his wisdom thought I ought to be working with in the secular world. There was a day approaching when I would be released from labouring among these 'high-tech pagans' and I looked forward to it with great anticipation.

No longer would I be forced to hear the Lord's name dragged through the mud or be asked where Cain got his wife. Nor should I have to be the brunt of any more stupid jokes from the head of my department. He pointed out to me one day that all of his immediate staff members represented minorities, saying that one was black, one oriental, and so forth. I said 'What about Andy?' He said, 'Andy is an alcoholic which only leaves you and you're a Christian.'

Possibly you have already guessed that my anticipation was ill-founded. It was only a few short months before people would ask me how I enjoyed 'full time Christian service'. My reply was, 'It would be fine if it wasn't for the Christians.' No, I didn't have to hear the same language or bad jokes, but I found that some Christians simply can't be depended upon and others seem to be professional gossips. I was shocked at the 'professional jealousy' that added a spirit of competition. (Especially when I found it in myself.)

Naturally these things existed in the secular world with greater frequency, but there was a difference. Christians are more covert. Having someone attempting to 'cut your throat' in the secular world is expected and in a peculiar way almost respected. It is almost as though there were a Geneva Convention for the 'asphalt jungle'—or honour among thieves.

In the Christian world such manifestations of our old sin nature are simply not allowed—nor should they be. However, the fact that Christians should behave markedly differently makes it easy to feel one is operating in a 'germ-free environment' and that just isn't so. We are still all humans and we still lose control of our old natures. The fact that we are only human doesn't make getting hurt any easier to bear. The wounds we receive at the hands of other believers seem to go a lot deeper. Perhaps it's because we are so much more vulnerable to other believers. One book I read contained two pages of occupations listed in order of their stress potential; 'clergy' was near the bottom. That should give clergy families a good laugh.

The fact that one finds it difficult to share without sounding like a cry baby means that they are probably not going to get the support or sound advice they need. Being realistic, it is difficult to talk about the fact that someone is gossiping about you without sounding like a gossip yourself. It is not a matter of whether to suffer the slings and arrows of outrageous fortune or go back into secular work. It isn't either/or—smile and take it, or quit. Pain has a purpose. It is a sign of healthy life. This type of pain is as much a symptom of something requiring attention as is physical pain. We won't profit from the pain by attempting to ignore it. If nothing else pain will make us more sensitive. We would know it was more realistic to listen a lot more before we start giving advice.

There is a reason why pastors, in particular, sometimes fall into the trap of hammering away with what often seems simplistic admonitions such as 'You're seated in the heavenlies.' I call it the 'loop-hole theory'. Just as clever accountants find loop holes in tax laws to the benefit of their clients and lawyers search for loop holes in the law to have their clients acquitted, some Christians believe there are loop holes in God's promises. Even if they don't actually believe there are loop holes they tend to handle the truth as if they thought someone else would see a 'loop hole'.

It works like this: A pastor begins to recognise, for instance, that God wants to do a lot more healing in his congregation than has been the case, but no one is looking to God for healing. So he quite naturally begins to preach on the subject.

He may recognise that, although we expect far too little from God in this area, God does not heal every time someone of faith prays for a healing. He also knows that the healing is the responsibility of God and not our own— all we can do is ask. The pastor is certainly aware that God allows some people to suffer afflictions for reasons that he alone understands, because he alone knows his plan.

But the pastor also knows his people—or he thinks he does. He thinks they are not easily moved to faith. So his strategy is to preach healing as an open-ended miracle that needs only to be plugged into. This places the responsibility for obtaining a healing squarely on the shoulders of the believer. It means they will be much more motivated to get to grips with appropriating their healing.

He is afraid that if he broaches the fact that God doesn't always heal just because we pray, they will see it as a loop hole in the promise. If they spot this loop hole they will all slip through it, never once expecting God to heal. He sees the best way of avoiding this loop hole is to focus on their responsibility. Any doubts can be labelled a lack of faith, and failures can be blamed on a lack of faith as well.

Prosperity has been given exactly the same treatment. 'The reason you're not driving a Rolls Royce is because you only have Mini faith.' Almost anything in the Bible can be subject to this over-simplification. 'Rejoice in the Lord always' is a hard command to argue with, but we are to weep with those who weep and mourn with those who mourn. Solomon tells us there is a time to weep and a time to laugh, a time to mourn and a time to dance. Consequently even this 'air tight' statement requires some interpretation.

However, we are afraid that if we agree that there are times when we may accept that we have legitimate fears, doubts, feelings of depression and even bitterness or hatred, we will have created a loop hole for everyone to crawl through. This results in a group of people who are totally dishonest with themselves and at the same time encouraging their neighbour to the same self-deception.

The promises of God do form an authoritative basis for

dealing with these negative emotions, but there is a fair distance between ministering emotional healing from a factual basis and handing out scriptures on a cliché level. By the cliché level, I mean saying 'In everything give thanks,' in the same way one might say 'Have a nice day.' We, the church, have given and accepted the promises of God at the cliché level to the extent that we have little or no intellectual grasp of the truth.

Josh McDowell has been quoted as saying, 'History shows that when a generation fails to know why they believe what they do, their convictions are in danger of being undermined.' Giving or even trying to act on advice at such a superficial level is the fast road to faith that amounts to nothing more than group conformity behaviour (doing what is acceptable).

This in turn means we are ill-equipped to deal with the pressures of life and light years away from being able to minister to those who are hurting. This inability to appropriate the truth realistically means we are prime candidates for stress. With a limited number of possible exceptions that we will discuss later, Christians should expect to suffer the same pressures experienced by non-Christians.

But if God's plan for life doesn't equip us to deal more effectively with those pressures, either God has nothing to offer towards effective living or we don't know how to apply it.

When I mentioned earlier that it was possible to have legitimate emotions such as bitterness or hatred, some may have winced in disbelief. I didn't say that those feelings were to be encouraged, condoned or even that they were right, but they could nevertheless be legitimate. Personally, I don't believe I ever hated or was bitter toward someone without a legitimate reason. However,

God demands that we hand our legitimate grievances over to him. Failure to do so is sin, but it is a sin that we cannot be cajoled out of with a cliché level admonition.

The very fact that the Christian life is a journey tells us that even God, who will tolerate no sin, recognises that obedience will not be instantaneous in some areas. Surrendering bitterness to God is absolutely mandatory, but I believe there is sufficient evidence in the Bible that God has a lot of patience with us while we are suffering—a lot more than we have with each other and sometimes more than we have with ourselves.

3

Pressure Is Not A Synonym For Stress

Stress is a physical response to a perceived threat. That threat, whether an on-coming car or the loss of our job, is what we are referring to as pressure. When circumstances make it necessary to have your married children move in with you, it brings pressure. A wrong response to that pressure introduces stress. The first baby, as big a blessing as it is, brings a certain amount of pressure. Financial problems bring pressure. Raising children through the 'terrible twos' produces pressure as do their teenage years. None of these things automatically produces stress. Stress is determined by our response to these pressures of life.

The Bible doesn't promise us life without pressure, but it does show us God's natural order for dealing with pressure without stress.

Society is beginning to come to grips with ecology because it is a matter of physical science, but dealing with our psychological environment is another matter. In a recent radio panel discussion it was stated that ecological considerations must be given priority over economic and quality-of-life issues because the latter were of the man-made world and the man-made world is contingent upon the existence of a natural world. Therefore, since the man-made world cannot exist without the natural world it must yield the right of way.

This is true in the physical realm and there is a similar dynamic in the non-physical world.

Mental peace and stability cannot be maintained indefinitely while ravaging the spiritual environment.

Just as the tolerance of the environment is not based on the values, desires or requirements of any one individual or group but on certain fixed absolutes, so is the non-physical world.

Society has abandoned the idea of moral and ethical absolutes in favour of relativism. At first, this seemed to have no more adverse effect than throwing a coke can out of the car window and was equally as convenient. There is some evidence that society is beginning to recognise that even the non-physical highways are becoming an eye-sore. But there is little to suggest that they have made the connection between the mess and the throwing of cans out of the car, metaphorically speaking. That is to say, they haven't connected the vast array of psychological problems including the increase of suicide, divorce and stress with the abandonment of absolutes.

The current preoccupation with stress is one of the symptoms of a society that has violated the natural law long enough to feel the repercussions. The problem is finding a solution in a society that bases its logic on the concept that there is no God. Relativism, the obvious result of excluding God, maintains there is no such thing as moral right or wrong, only acceptable and unacceptable. Relativism insists there is no such thing as objective truth and implies that claims to absolute truth are a form of bigotry. Relativism is tolerant of all ideas except the idea that God has spoken and therefore there are absolutes. It will not tolerate that.

This means that life is an experiment. The only way to find how it should be lived is to experiment and see what works. The problem is that what seems to work today is inconsistent with tomorrow's findings and so it takes a long time. The Christian problem is that we tend to borrow too many experiment results from the secular world. We should know many of these results will eventually be found to be wrong because they directly contradict God's law.

Some pressure in this life can be avoided. Most of it must

be accepted as we accept seeds as an integral part of tomatoes. Just as many of us might find eating tomatoes without any of the seeds a bit bland or tasteless, so would be a life completely devoid of pressure. We actually need a certain amount of pressure to be productive. The way we deal with pressure determines the richness of our life.

We have no dispute with the scientific world over the actual nature and function of stress. But we have considerable differences over how to deal with it. These issues are fundamental to the question of whether stress prevention is possible or whether our efforts might more realistically be invested in simply coping with stress. We believe it can be prevented.

Stress is like an immigrant with dual citizenship, having its residence in the physical world but its origins in the non-physical world.

This allows it to serve as a liaison between our psychological and physical beings. Its function is to marshal the body's resources to deal effectively with emergencies involving a physical response. The classic definition of stress in everyday language is:

> An alarm function of the sympathetic nervous system, causing increased blood pressure to major active muscles at the same time decreasing blood flow to organs not involved in rapid activity.

This does not define stress as an influence which is 'out in the world'; it is our physical response to various influences from the outside world.

There are times when it is convenient to be in such a state of emergency alertness. Most of us find times when our state of emergency readiness far outstrips the actual physical demands of the emergency. For instance we may read something in the newspaper which 'makes our blood boil'. Needless to say our blood is not boiling, but we are experiencing increased blood pressure to major active muscles at the same time decreasing blood flow to organs not involved in rapid activity. We are 'combat ready'; we are in a state of readiness to flee from danger or to attack an opponent.

It may seem perfectly normal to feel a bit acrimonious while reading an article which compared Billy Graham and all he stands for with the late Ayatollah and all he stood for. But does it really take increased flow to the major muscles to write a letter to the editor? The problem is we don't find it easy to train our sympathetic nervous systems to distinguish between writing to the editor and punching him on the nose.

This presents a problem. Most people find excess stress uncomfortable to say the least. It causes headaches, tummy aches, back aches and shortness of breath. Not only is it uncomfortable, it is dangerous. It can cause ulcers, diverticulitis, arthritis, heart attacks, strokes and literally hundreds of other physical problems. In other words, it costs us to get our systems all fired up if we don't burn off the energy. This tension provided for fight or flight can actually wear out the very system it was designed to protect. It does help to burn off excess energy through a good workout at the gym, but that doesn't address the more basic problem.

It needs to be pointed out for clarification that books on stress are not usually concerned with normal, desirable functions of the sympathetic nervous system. This book is about *excess* stress and we will be limiting the use of the word stress to the undesirable excess, ie, Stress = excess stress.

Not only does stress have physical repercussions, it also creates problems in our relationships. Stress inhibits our ability to respond appropriately to others, placing them under pressure. That pressure in turn makes them vulnerable to stress. This gives stress somewhat of a contagious quality. However, before we accept that it is like the black plague we should examine the component factors influencing this physical reaction.

Factors influencing stress are:

Pressure (real or perceived);
Our ability to deal with pressure;
Our support system.

Pressure and our ability to deal with it are somewhat more evident than what is meant by a support system. In this case our support system is generally our family, friends, church and possibly even our working colleagues; those who provide support and encouragement.

Jim Phillips had been on the receiving end of some pretty rotten treatment from his boss. Fortunately his wife Catherine stood by his side as did his colleagues.

Martin and Sue Smith's new daughter was Down's Syndrome and had several complications. He was a member of the US Air Force stationed in England, which meant their families were in the US. Fortunately, they were members of an extremely sharing, caring church fellowship.

Jane Ellis' husband had gone off with another woman and her house group leader and his wife had made themselves available to support her in any way possible. They were her support system as were Jim Phillips' wife and colleagues to him and the Smiths' church to them.

Almost any relationship can serve as an integral part of our support system. As the title of this book implies our marriage can serve as the backbone of our support system or it can be our main source of pressure. We feel a good goal for married couples is to have their marriage relationship in such a state that both partners consider it to be the most reliable human element in their support system.

Our ability to deal with pressure is, and has been, the subject of extensive research, which has required some way to calibrate amounts of pressure. One of these attempts to give value to various situations creating pressure is the Holmes-Rahe scale. This scale has been referred to or has appeared in nearly every book on the subject since it was published in 1967. We are including it because it gives some indication of this effort.

HOLMES-RAHE STRESS SCALE

Thomas H. Holmes and Richard Rahe, Stress Rating Scale,
Journal of Psychosomatic Research, 1967, Volume II, page 26

Event	Value Score
Death of spouse	100
Divorce	73
Marital separation	65
Jail term	63
Death of close family member	63
Personal injury or illness	53
Marriage	50
Fired from work	47
Marital reconciliation	45
Retirement	45
Change in family member's health	44
Pregnancy	40
Sex difficulties	39
Addition to family	39
Business readjustment	39
Change in financial status	38
Death of close friend	37
Change in number of marital arguments	35
Mortgage or loan over $10,000	31
Foreclosure of mortgage or loan	30
Change in work responsibilities	29
Son or daughter leaving home	29
Trouble with in-laws	29
Outstanding personal achievement	28
Spouse begins or starts work	26
Starting or finishing school	26
Change in living conditions	25
Revision of personal habits	24
Trouble with boss	23
Change in work hours, conditions	20
Change in residence	20
Change in schools	20
Change in recreational habits	19
Change in church activities	19
Change in social activities	18
Mortgage or loan under $10,000	18

Change in sleeping habits	16
Change in number of family gatherings	15
Change in eating habits	15
Vacation	13
Christmas season	12
Minor violation of the law	11

We are including the Holmes-Rahe scale mainly as a beginning point in discussing pressure. There is nothing really scientific about it, nor can there be since it attempts to assign objective values to concrete circumstances, which in real life hold extremely subjective values. Take for instance the top situation 'Death of a spouse'. Certainly that is a heavy burden; in many cases 100 points would not be sufficient. On the other hand, placing it in an Agatha Christie context, the man who was about to murder his wife suddenly learning she has been killed in a road accident might have difficulty concealing his relief.

Perhaps even more unscientific is the title that has been assigned to it: The Holmes-Rahe Stress Rating Scale. This is a step in the direction of confusing pressure with stress.

Pressure is nearly always an outside force and generally beyond our control. Stress is our reaction to this outside force, or even more accurately, it is a reaction to our perception of this outside force.

There are obviously a lot more sources of pressure than this list suggests. We live in a very pressurised society. One factor which is the catalyst for much of our pressure is opportunity. Rapid transportation, labour saving devices and fast food have provided the opportunity to get in so much more living in a life time than was possible a few generations back. We have greater quality of life opportunities and greater opportunity to vary our experiences. All of these opportunities bring with them decisions and the fear of making wrong decisions. These decisions frequently entail change, and you will note the word 'change' appears quite frequently on the stress scale. They also bring with them the urgency to move quickly so as not to miss out on any opportunities. We then have the pressure of decisions and change compounded by 'the tyranny of the urgent'.

Some of this pressure can be avoided by simply getting things into proper perspective. Learning to say no to opportunities that will overcrowd our life avoids pressure. Good management helps as well, but there are plenty of pressures in life that can't be avoided or scheduled. Many of the things listed on the Holmes-Rahe scale fall into that category.

According to Drs Thomas Holmes and Richard Rahe if you score less than 150 points in a year you have only a 37% chance of becoming ill in the next two years. Between 150 and 300 brings your possibilities to 51%, but over 300 brings your chances to 80%. What this tells you is that adverse physical reactions tend to occur in direct proportion to the psychological pressure that is experienced. There is a link. What it doesn't tell you is why this happens. It fails to explain why some people fall apart at 150 points while others go whistling through in excess of 400. Obviously pressure isn't the only factor. There is still our support system and our ability to handle pressure to examine.

Unfortunately we don't have much control over our support system either. The nearest thing we have to control is 'the golden rule'. We can be as supportive as possible but there is no guarantee that those whom we support will be supportive of us when it comes to the crunch. In fact depending on others for support that they either can't or won't give, actually multiplies stress.

I don't mean by this that families and marriages are not to be interdependent units. They should be, but that can't be the only arrow in our quiver in our battle against stress. The marriage partner that we rightly depend on as the key factor in our support system may be critically ill. Situations can occur which virtually neutralise our entire support system. Just as Martin and Sue Smith were unfortunate enough to have a Down's Syndrome baby thousands of miles from their extended family, others have found themselves in marital difficulties with no one to turn to, not even a caring church. Survival in such situations depends on factors other than a support system.

The final factor is our ability to handle pressure. Ability factors consist of *personality*, *general health*, and our *system of dealing with stress*.

Psychologists and physiologists attempting to isolate qualities which seem to give some individuals greater ability to deal with stress acknowledge certain personality types have a definite advantage. We are all aware of certain choleric individuals who seem to be victims of a temperament that drags them through life looking like the film world stereotype of a Regimental Sergeant Major with blood vessels permanently puffed on their neck and forehead. In professional circles these people are known as 'type A's. We know of others who have never been rattled in their entire lives—nothing fazes them. The latter are far less apt to suffer from stress than the former—not through any achievement of their own but simply an advantage of nature. This advantage is no more an accomplishment than never having to wear glasses or the ability to eat anything without gaining weight (against which there should be a law).

It is also obvious that some people's bodies can tolerate more abuse before they begin showing symptoms of stress. Some people seem to be made out of pressure-tested, heat-resistant material which allows them to go around with the blood vessels poked out on their neck day in day out with no observable repercussions. Others suffer from what we used to refer to as PPP—particularly poor protoplasm. A good sneeze would cause a nose bleed and real verbal hostility would put them in hospital. Tension headaches and upset stomachs are nearly as common as meals for this type.

These are inherited factors. We cannot take credit for positive ones or totally rely on them, neither should we allow ourselves to be victimised by the negative traits if we happen to have been short-changed. We may be disadvantaged by health or temperament, but disadvantage is a long way from defeat.

We are not accountable for our genetic makeup but the way we choose to respond to pressure is definitely our personal responsibility.

A lot of research has been conducted to answer the question of why some people seem to tolerate far more pressure than others. Most of the evidence seems to point to the individual's system of dealing with pressure rather than inherited immunity. In searching for 'stress survival', the only factor we really have control over is our system of dealing with pressure. Scoring 300 Holmes-Rahe points is not an automatic authorisation for a 'nervous breakdown' or a trip to hospital. A nervous breakdown is mainly an indication that our system for coping with pressure has proved inadequate for the amount of trials life is dealing to us. Certainly it is easier to avoid a breakdown when we are in the peak of health than when we are sickly. And people who are naturally 'hyper' require greater self-discipline to respond any other way than simply going 'ballistic'.

The Christian system of dealing with pressure is simply God's plan for living. That may sound simplistic but listen to what the Bible says about it.

> His divine power has given us everything we need for life and godliness through our knowledge of him who called us by his own glory and goodness. Through these he has given us his very great and precious promises, so that through them you may participate in the divine nature and escape the corruption in this world caused by evil desires (2 Pet 1:3–5).

'Everything we need for life and godliness', 'participate in the divine nature and escape the corruption in this world' would be tall statements from any other source, but because they come to us on good authority they offer the ultimate in hope. Naturally we cannot earth these statements without specifics, but there are some very specific principles provided.

2 Timothy 3:16–17 says that 'All Scripture is God-breathed and is useful for teaching, rebuking, correcting

and training in righteousness, so that the man of God may be thoroughly equipped for every good work.'

The Bible teaches us these principles and it rebukes us when we fail to apply them, but it doesn't just leave us there. It provides another set of principles for correction.

Violation of this plan causes repercussions ultimately producing stress. Stress can be alleviated through applying God's plan.

The most pertinent specifics of God's plan will be discussed in part three. However, part two contains valuable insights to why even those conversant with God's plan are frequently defeated in their attempts at applying it.

The exercises at the end of this and some following chapters were adapted from a stress action pack designed by Dr Bill Munro of the Stress And Life Trust. They represent Christian beliefs applied to the latest in stress research and are used in this book by his consent. The complete pack may be obtained by writing to: SALT, The Istana, Freezeland Lane, Bexhill-on-Sea, East Sussex TN39 5JD, England.

FACTS AND ACTION

THE FOLLOWING ARE TYPICAL EFFECTS OF STRESS OR STRAIN

However, they may have other causes and it is wise to have a check up from your doctor to exclude physical conditions.

Feeling down	Sleeping badly	Loss of appetite
On edge	Nightmares	Excessive eating
Irritable	Fainting spells	Trembling
Cry easily	Giddy spells	Laugh nervously
Want to run & hide	Need to urinate frequently	Difficult to concentrate
Stuttering	Sweat easily	Can't get breath
Easily startled by small noises	Difficult to make decisions	Difficulty in swallowing
Forget things	Dry mouth	No energy
Put things off	Lump in the throat	Easily tired
Fidgeting	Nail biting	Lack of sex drive
Impulsive behaviour (prima donna)		

MENTAL, EMOTIONAL AND BEHAVIOURAL EFFECTS

Anxiety	Alcoholism	Depression
Phobias	Smoking more	Feel helpless
Panic attacks	Addictions	Feel a failure
Hysteria	Hypochondria	Giving up
Nervous breakdown		

PSYCHOSOMATIC EFFECTS

Some forms of:

Asthma	Backache	Hay fever
Neck pain	Allergies	Shoulder pain

Dysmennorhoea
Migraine
Spastic colon
Heartburn
Premenstrual
   tension

Excema, rashes
Frigidity
Irritable colon
Diarrhoea
Tinnitus (ringing in
   the ears)

Impotence
Headaches
Constipation
Indigestion

PHYSICAL EFFECTS

High blood
   pressure
Lowered immunity
Infections
Cancer

Hormone
   problems
Chronic pain
Arthritis
Overactive thyroid

Ischaemic heart
   disease
Angina
Diabetes
Peptic ulcer

SPIRITUAL EFFECTS

Dryness
Depression

Using the list of Effects of Stress shown above, circle the number in Questions a—e which best describes your recent experience (in the last year or so).

EFFECTS OF STRESS

1 = none
2 = very slight
3 = slight
4 = moderate
5 = severe
6 = very severe

I have been experiencing:
a) Vague Effects of Stress   1 2 3 4 5 6
b) Mental/Emotional/Behavioural Effects of Stress   1 2 3 4 5 6
c) Psychosomatic Effects of Stress   1 2 3 4 5 6
d) Physical Effects of Stress   1 2 3 4 5 6
e) Spiritual Effects of Stress   1 2 3 4 5 6
                                                  Months in the past year
f) I have taken tranquillisers for   0 1 2 3 4 5 6

g) I have taken sleeping pills for   0 1 2 3 4 5 6
                                        Times in the past year
h) I have consulted my doctor for effects of stress 0 1 2 3 4 5 6
i) I have seen a specialist for effects of stress   0 1 2 3 4 5 6

If you have scored many 4s, 5s or 6s and there is no physical cause, it suggests that you have been suffering from quite severe effects of stress or strain.

Scores in the mid-range, especially in Questions a–e suggest mild to moderate degrees of stress.

Ideally you should be scoring consistently at the low end of the scale.

HIGH SCORERS—

DO NOT WORRY—By seeking God's truth and applying it you can improve your score and more importantly your ability to live successfully without fear of stress.

LOW SCORERS—

GOOD—By understanding the basic truths regarding stress you will know how to keep in the low scores and continue to live more successfully without fear of stress.

HELPING OTHERS—

You can help others deal with the effects of stress by encouraging them in practical application of their faith as well as some of these exercises.

Part Two

GOD'S BASIC STRESS PREVENTION

4

Some Distorted Basics

When Mary Eckerd's five year old suffered multiple fractures as the result of being hit by a car, her neighbour said: *'There is no such thing as a personal loving God*, because he wouldn't have allowed this.'

Bill Stone led his church's prison ministry and had been working with an inmate who was growing by leaps and bounds. When he mentioned it to the warden he said: *'People don't change, they only adapt.'*

Eveline Green's daughter was living with her boyfriend. Nothing she said could convince her daughter to do otherwise. Eveline was so distraught over the matter that her doctor placed her on Valium saying: *'When an individual experiences a lack of control they will develop a proportionate level of stress.'*

Juliet Lynch was extremely upset that an underprivileged sixteen year old boy whom she taught in school was going to have to serve time due to repeated drug offences. She didn't think he was really responsible for the mess he was in, and said: *'We are all victims of our genetic and environmental programming.'*

All four of these italicised statements are very common and they are logical. Logic is simply to use the available information to reach a conclusion, solve a problem or plan a course of action. Each of the above statements is a logical conclusion if one doesn't believe in God or believe what he says about himself. The basic values involved in reaching

53

conclusions determine our world view. These four statements are typical of a secular world view.

The problem is that too many Christians, at least par-
tially, accept some or all of these statements. When we do
so we are unwittingly adopting a secular world view to deal
with that area of life. In so doing we become more vulnerable to the pressures of life. Perhaps it is because the
statements are made by well qualified, well meaning
people—people who are revered in society. We forget that
the most brilliant mind in the world cannot come to the
correct conclusion if it is missing a part of the equation.
And God is the key factor in these equations. Most of the
time we accept these types of statements because we simply
don't think them through. We don't realise that they contradict a Christian world view.

These four opening statements are missing vital information which the Bible makes abundantly clear from cover to
cover. They are so basic to applying Christianity in every
day life that we call them *basic basics*.

THE BASIC BASICS

- *God is love*
- *His agenda for his children is to develop the character of Christ.*
- *God is in control—he never takes a holiday from his responsibilities.*
- *He never gives us a holiday. We are always respons-ible for right behaviour.*

You may want to know why the list is limited to only
four—after all there are a lot more basics regarding the
character and plan of God. There are several reasons to
pick these four. They seem to be the facts with which the
world is most often at war. They are the factors most
frequently involved in the problems that bring Christian
couples in for counselling, and, for some strange reason,

they seem to be the facts most frequently glossed over or distorted in Christian writings.

We believe that having a firm grasp on these basics is essential to stress prevention. As we unpack them it will become clear that their significance lies in the fact that they are pillars of our faith. As such they are the foundation for the more specific principles which form the framework for effective marriage relationships (and all other relationships for that matter) and keep us from converting pressure into stress.

It is our relationship with God in the vertical plane which provides us with the strength to handle the pressures which arise in our horizontal relationships.

The strength to stand up under pressure is obviously a matter of faith. Faith requires understanding; not just information or knowledge, but understanding.

A friend of mine is an engineer. He has milling machines, lathes, drill presses and a lot of other pieces of equipment I couldn't name. He is also very good at his trade. He works hard but if I need a part made for something he is never so far behind that he can't find the time. And he is pleased to do so because he loves me as a brother. I have another brother who is equally as skilled, has sufficient equipment and who also loves me. Unfortunately, he is always backlogged with work and just simply doesn't have the time. I understand the situations of both of these men so when I have a need I go to the first one. I know he can and will solve my problem.

My understanding of the situation isn't based on hearsay: 'Just see old Charley, he'll be glad to knock one of those out for you.' It is based on repeated experience and my personal knowledge of the man. I know he likes doing that type of work, I know he finds the little jobs I bring in a welcome diversion from his routine work and I also know, from both my experience and his reputation, he likes helping people. So he is the person I turn to when I have that type of problem.

The fact that we, as Christians, have a similar understanding of God means that there are particular situations where we can approach God with near certainty of his full co-operation. I am not sure he will be excited about my request for a new BMW, but when I ask for strength to stand or wisdom in meeting someone's needs I know I have his full attention. I know this because my understanding of the character of God tells me that he, like my engineer friend, also likes helping people and particularly when they are attempting to develop Christ-like character qualities. I know, for instance, that asking God to help me around a problem is never as sure a proposition as asking for his strength through a problem.

Joyce frequently tells of the time she was giving God a list of things that were wrong with me, asking him to change them. (This was years ago I must point out.) She only got about half way through when God said, 'Why don't you turn David over to me and let's just concentrate on you?' She said she knew that had to be God because that wasn't something she would say to herself, and now, after years of studying the heart and mind of God, she also knows that is exactly the type of thing he would say in that type of situation.

God is love

On the first issue, everyone knows God's chief attribute is love—even those who don't believe in him. That's why they always trot out statements such as—'If God is love why did he allow this to happen?' What they fail to grasp is what he means by love. Most of us have a bit of a problem with that. When we hear 'God is love' we tend to think of some sort of a celestial Father Christmas who goes around bestowing gifts. That's not the message God intended to convey with that term. We forget the Hebrews 12 facet of God's love which involves his discipline and training.

The description 'God is love' means that he has our long range wellbeing constantly in focus; that he is willing to hit us with a plank if that's what it takes to get our attention. We're sure that he would view the resultant knot on our head simply as an acceptable inconvenience. It doesn't always compute in our earthbound thinking to say 'God is love, and he let me get a speeding ticket. God is love and my child has been sick at home for two weeks requiring my wife to miss work to stay home and look after him.'

One cannot always prove that God is love by the circumstances, but we can accept the circumstances because we know God is love.

Each of us has had experiences in our lives where, in retrospect, we could easily see what appeared to be a calamity, turn out to be a blessing. But most of us would be quick to admit that we still have some unsolved mysteries. We still cannot understand why God allowed it to happen.

It isn't easy to believe in a loving God when we know of no reason why we should be suffering. At least, it goes against our human reasoning. However, many people have been through some very trying experiences and found that God was showing them the exact state of their faith. Peter says that God allows trials so that our faith may be proved genuine—or may be proved to be pretty shoddy. In which case God is really doing us a favour because without faith we are naked. This is what this chapter is all about—faith. And the basics are the pillars which support our faith under the pressures of life.

As near as we know we weren't in sin or planning any the day our daughter-in-law phoned to announce that our twenty-nine-year-old son had been instantly killed in a car crash. But all of a sudden we were faced with a decision either to judge God by the circumstances or judge the circumstances by God. Is God the being he states he is in his word or do I allow the circumstances to convince me otherwise? Has God rejected us? No, he says he will never forsake us.

We still haven't any better idea of his purpose in Bill's death than we did at the time. We have ideas for a few somewhat comforting conjectures, but nothing that comes near making it worthwhile in our eyes. Bill is with his heavenly Father who loves him and may even be privy to the reason he left so early. He's all right. Our choices seem to be to accept that God is love or to bitterly attack his character. (Love is one of the character qualities he wants to be known by.) We chose to believe him. We personally know a lot of people who have been through exactly the same experience and the Bible records couples like Adam and Eve and David and Bathsheba who lost children and still believed God is love.

The practical conclusion to be reached by understanding this long-range, no-holds-barred type of love is: God is love, therefore we can accept his agenda as being the best for us.

His agenda for his children is to develop the character of Christ

The second basic, developing the character of Christ, is exactly what Romans 8:29 is all about—'being conformed to the image of his Son'. We may understand God's goal is that we develop the character of Christ, but we frequently fail to recognise that it means he is more committed to our character than our comfort.

The value system in God's economy is based on character, not money or the things it can buy. Silver, gold, and precious stones are mentioned a lot in the Bible but mainly as an allegorical value system—like when compared with wood, hay and stubble in 1 Corinthians 3:12. It can cause a serious twist in our theology if we get this one wrong.

It is easy to develop a gospel of prosperity if we believe that God's concerns are the same as our concerns. But if we do, it is because we have created God in our image.

Materialism is definitely a problem of our day and time, but it is not the thing that brings most people for counselling. Most people come for counselling because they are extremely uncomfortable, and most of them are uncomfortable in relationships. In fact, most people have to be extremely uncomfortable before they will see a counsellor. The problem is that most of them expect that the counsellor will make them comfortable. The fact is that discomfort is not their problem, it is only a symptom of their real problem.

When couples come for counselling we tell them that if they are only interested in relieving the discomfort, it is doubtful if we can be of much help to them. But we quickly add that if they would like to explore this situation to see what opportunities it presents for their personal growth as Christians, we can probably be of assistance.

That could sound to some like a pretty hard-nosed approach. After all, shouldn't we relieve suffering regardless of the person's Christian commitment? Surely Jesus didn't ask people to sign a pledge before healing them. Certainly we would be willing to help our non-Christian neighbours through a rough place with no spiritual demands, just as Jesus provided physical healings. But when Jesus was confronted with non-physical situations such as with Nicodemus or the 'rich young ruler' his approach was much more radical. These were religious men with spiritual problems.

There are quite a number of counselling methods designed to solve life's problems without having to consider God or his plan at all, but we aren't really trained in them. However, the very fact that these schools of counselling exist (over 250 of them), is proof that secular man is not interested in God's plan. Therefore, there is little chance that our non-Christian neighbours would come to us for help in the first place. Our primary concern is with couples who claim to be Christians but can't seem to apply Christianity in their marriage. And chances are slim that a secular counsellor will be able to reach to the root of their problem.

There is more evidence that God is behind their current discomfort than there is for his concern in clearing it up. His main concern is dealing with the root problem—sin (usually some form of selfishness). The discomfort is merely a symptom. Most of life's problems are the direct result of violating God's principles. Certainly others sin against us causing us problems as well, but even here our response is the key factor in determining the magnitude of the problem. This cause-and-effect dynamic was evidently set in motion by God in order to move us along toward his objective—that we develop the character of Christ.

Our familiarity with these basics has a cumulative effect on our ability to face life, because they are building blocks in our understanding of God. For example, to question: 'If God is love why doesn't he take care of all the pain and suffering in the world?' we can answer: 'His agenda is not that the human race might be comfortable for their three score years and ten, but that they might know him throughout eternity, and knowing him, be like him.'

God is in control—he never takes a holiday from his responsibilities

Thirdly, the doctrine of the sovereignty of God means he is always in control and he has the necessary power to bring about his plan. If we really understood the sovereignty of God and his goal for our lives we would be much quicker to associate the trials of life which come our way with God's plan to develop the character of Christ in our lives. We would stop asking, 'Why me?' and possibly ask, 'What are you trying to teach me Lord?'

Certainly everything is not a character lesson for the person involved, but everything is a part of God's plan. Some of the unpleasant things God allows to come into our lives may well be as a ministry to others. The world complains of the remoteness of God, but he frequently overcomes this by demonstrating his strength and character through the lives of his saints. We might well ask, 'How does this fit into your plan Lord?'

A word of caution: Some Christians give the impression that personal disasters are somehow 'sanctified' only when' the purpose has been discovered. We are quite sure God takes no offence at his purposes being questioned by those involved in suffering, but there are ways of asking questions. 'Now why in the world did you do that?' usually means 'That wasn't very bright.' Directed toward God such questioning would not only show a lack of faith in his sovereignty, but disrespect as well.

Conversely, asking in faith is simply to say 'I know you have a purpose and it would be comforting to know where all this fits in.' There is, however, no guarantee that he will show us. In fact it must be, more often than not, that to do so would require a major complex revelation of God's plans; much more than would be profitable.

Having faith in the fact that God is in control does not rule out pain. Grief is not a sign of spiritual immaturity. The idea that Christians should be bright and breezy while suffering pain and loss is as hideous a distortion of the truth as the notion that Christianity has nothing to offer at such times.

Our son Bill was a big robust fishing boat captain whom we frequently compared with Peter, and in whom, as parents, we had similar hopes. Losing him in the prime of his life wasn't easy, but we had a pattern to follow. Job had no idea that God was developing the script for a book on the sovereignty of God when he took all Job's children away. The book of Job was written to demonstrate specifically the absolute control of the God who 'is love', and yet most of the book is devoted to some of the worst calamities that can possibly befall a human.

Job's sufferings were definitely a part of God's plan to show future generations that God is always in control.

We don't find it the least bit odd that the God who wants to be known as loving spent a whole book showing his control over the events of life. He wanted us to know exactly how deep that love is and the value system under which that love is measured. And he wanted us to know that when trials come in life, there hasn't been some dreadful mistake. God was definitely not out to lunch when we married the person we married. He wasn't on holiday when we were notified that the man we felt was the reincarnation of Atilla the Hun would be our new boss. Nor was the heavenly computer down for repairs when the Hell's Angels moved in next door. (Which actually happened to a Christian family in London.)

The world often sees the things that rocket one person into prominence over his or her peers as a quirk of fate. But are these things quirks? Joni Erickson Tada would most likely have been one more attractive middle-aged, middle-class American Christian woman, awash in a sea of mediocre middle-class Christianity. Instead, God got her attention through a broken neck and her paralysed body has become the platform to reach millions. Her message is that God is with us through trials. He is not simply standing on the other side waiting for us to come through.

There are other parallels between Joni and Job. Job had friends who told him that his problems were the result of sin in his life and we have heard the same thing said about Joni. 'The reason God doesn't heal her is because she either lacks the faith or there is unconfessed sin in her life.' Such people have missed some very basic truths about God's character and his agenda.

Please note: I did not say God broke Joni's neck, but I did say something which is extremely close. As we understand from Job, Satan cannot cause any discomfort without God's permission. Jesus told his disciples in John 9 about the man born blind, saying 'This happened so that the work of God might be displayed in his life.'

Some people have the notion that saying God is sovereign means something like, he can effectively field any ball hit to him. In those terms it means much more than having control when the ball arrives; it means he had control over when it was hit and who hit it as well. God controls the batting order. He determines who will get to bat: Winston Churchill, Adolph Hitler, George Bush or Saddam Hussein.

Listen to the way Donald MacLeod, Professor of Systematic Theology, Free Church College, Edinburgh describes it.

> The most basic of all Christian convictions is that God exists; and exists as a God in sovereign control. That means a control which is both macrocosmic and microcosmic. It extends to existence in all its forms and in all its magnitudes. Divine fore-ordination, divine preservation and divine government operate at the level of both astro-physics and micro-biology. That means that, as a theologian, I have to

believe that every single virus comes into being under the divine government. It doesn't exist unknown to God. It doesn't exist despite God. It doesn't exist in independence of God or beyond God. Its origination, its mutations and its development are all subject to the divine sovereignty.[1]

Certainly this is a cause and effect universe, but the God who created it to run that way is not limited by it. He intervenes and gives his angels the power to intervene in fulfilling his purposes.

We are considering these four basic truths together because each brings balance to our understanding of the others. It is not possible to grasp that a loving God allows such suffering as a broken neck until one has really come to grips with the priority God places on character. The fact that he loves us means he is committed to the proposition of developing the character of Christ in us and will use what ever means necessary.

However, if we lose sight of the importance God places on character, this affects our interpretation of calamities. We find we are either doubting his love or the amount of control he actually exercises. Having these three in focus helps us to understand the responsibility he places on us.

He never gives us a holiday. We are always responsible for right behaviour

Finally, he never gives us a holiday. We are always responsible for right behaviour. If we actually understood what a high priority our character is with God we would see trials as an integral part of the process rather than an excuse for *diminished responsibility*. We would not expect a holiday from righteousness even though we may have been sinned against. Occasionally even secular society recognises 'Success in life is not limited so much by the cards that are dealt us as it is by the way we play our hand.'

The doctrine of diminished responsibility was introduced in the garden when God asked Adam if he had eaten of the forbidden fruit. His reply was, 'It's that woman you gave me.' Eve said, 'It's the serpent who beguiled me.' The implication of this blameshifting was 'You can't actually hold us responsible considering all these extenuating circumstances, especially when you are responsible for the circumstances.' The important thing to learn is that it didn't work—God carried out his sentence as stated. None the less, this doctrine has been upheld by humankind ever since, as if it were legitimate.

Sigmund Freud gave it pseudo scientific status at the turn of the century with his school of psychoanalysis. This has tended to legitimise it to the point that with many it is a basic factor in their whole approach to life. This concept shows up everywhere. William Lee Wilbanks, in the December 1988 issue of *The Reader's Digest*, cited the case of a man convicted of having sexual intercourse with his fourteen-year-old stepdaughter. The judge placed the man on probation stating, 'Some men have a greater supply of male hormones that causes them to have much stronger sex urges than the normal male and they are much less able to resist temptation.'

The author of that article felt the four words which struck the most devastating blow to the very core of humanity were 'I can't help myself', stating 'This philosophy sees man as an organism being acted upon by biological and social forces rather than an agent with a free will. By ignoring the idea that people face temptations that can and should be resisted, it denies the very qualities that separate us from animals.'

Most of us would appreciate it if there were a doctrine of diminished responsibility. It runs against the grain of our fallen human nature to take full credit for our failures. Adam and Eve were not only the ancestors of all who would follow, they were representative of every human being who would enter this fallen world. As such, they gave a rather effective preview of the blame shifting that would continue throughout history.

There are two categories of people in particular who are not blessed by the knowledge that there is no such doctrine; 'victims' and 'controllers'. 'Victims' are people who view themselves as victims of life, and 'controllers', as the term implies, attempt to control everything and everyone. Both have a fairly low estimate of their own worth as people. The victim is fairly transparent about it because he thinks everyone knows he is sub standard. He is very pessimistic regarding his personal chances of success. The controller has a much better view of his chances in life because he is convinced he can keep others from finding out how worthless he is.

Some victims are looking for an excuse not to obey God. Some are looking for a way to excuse their failure to achieve in general and some of them are looking for a way to be comfortable with the fact that they have failed to reach what they perceive to be normal social expectations. They believe the fact that they have been victims of a troubled childhood, a broken home or over-strict toilet training meets the requirements of the doctrine of diminished responsibility.

Controllers are people whose main relationship technique is to control others. These people tend to have forceful personalities and are usually what psychologists term strong natural leaders. However, they don't actually make very good leaders until they learn to control their own controlling tendencies. We will discuss this type of person further in chapter eleven. The important thing here is to see how the way in which the controller invokes the doctrine of diminished responsibility differs from the victim's.

Controllers have less tendency to blame circumstances; they generally blame people. If you have ever worked on a project with a controller where something went wrong you probably had to bear the blame regardless of how obviously the fault seemed to lie with him/her. They are the type of people one always thinks should have been lawyers because they are so good at preparing their own defence.

The fact that this lie of diminished responsibility is so convincing, when it is so stupid, must mark it as one of the devil's masterpieces. It makes much more sense when things go wrong to begin our inquest by examining the things under our control rather than the things beyond our control. Examining first the factors beyond our control makes about as much sense as paying a TV repair man to come out and inform us that the set wasn't plugged in.

There is little or no hope in identifying failure factors which are beyond our control. But there is exciting hope when we identify failure factors which we can deal with.

There is hope in finding I am wrong. There is no hope in finding the world is wrong.

There is hope in discovering just exactly where I went wrong—I can correct it. Correcting the world is a bit more difficult.

We can't change the past or alter one single component of even our own personal history. We can frequently rectify past mistakes by correcting the damage caused by them. This can only be accomplished when we focus on the things within our scope of control rather than past history or what we wish others would do. Avoiding our individual responsibility is much more stress provoking than assuming it.

This concept is unpopular because it contains a potential 'guilt trip'. If someone is failing to respond appropriately to the trials of life and is suffering the resultant repercussions, he or she could be made to feel guilty by pointing out that their present dilemma is in fact a self-inflicted wound. However, our reticence to risk anyone feeling guilty has also removed hope from them and others. If they have no possibility for guilt it is because they are not responsible. If they, in fact, are not responsible it is because they have no control over the situation. If they have no control over the situation then they also have no hope of rectifying their situation or avoiding future recurrences.

Assuming responsibility for one's own failures does open the door to guilt, but God has made a way to deal with guilt. Facing responsibility and the possibility of having to deal with guilt is the only door available to real hope. Unfortunately, many Christians have absorbed a lethal dose of the secular notion that guilt is a problem.

The fact is that true moral guilt is not a problem at all; it is actually half of the solution.

It is half of the solution because it causes us to be

uncomfortable with our shortcomings. Indeed, if it weren't for guilt we wouldn't recognise them as shortcomings. They would be differences, irregularities, divergences or perhaps we would even take a more positive tack and call them our distinctives—anything but sin.

It is a very wonderful plan when one considers it. A loving God provides a manual for effective living. This consists of basic principles which, if violated, will have repercussions which could keep us from reaching the potential for which we were created. He then highlights the key principles in the form of specific commands. This means, when Jesus said, 'If you love me, you will obey what I command' (John 14:15) he wasn't simply setting an arbitrary standard for us to prove our love. He was saying it as the father of a young child would say, 'If you love me, don't play in the traffic.' The commands were designed with our interest at heart.

God has taken the step of separating these principles from mere cause-and-effect by adding a moral absolute, in the same way that governments enact laws against certain dangerous practices. The main difference is the government's judgement can be challenged. Frequently I find speed limits lowered to a very unnatural level, for no logical reason. I could complain to the authorities, because after all, it involves only human judgement. On the other hand, I may feel that God's ideas about, say, sexual conduct are too restrictive and take all the fun out of life. However, God's laws are made with perfect knowledge. We have to obey both laws, the ones we agree with and the ones we don't, but at least with God's laws we can relax in his judgement.

Feeling guilty is the first half of solving the problem. The next step is assuming responsibility for our own actions.

This is what it means to confess something. 1 John 1:9 says, 'If we confess our sins, he is faithful and just and will forgive us our sins and purify us from all unrighteousness.' Guilt need never be a problem to a believer. It was designed by a loving heavenly Father to draw us back to himself and he has made provision for the immediate elimination of it. However, we must never forget that this removal of guilt is contingent upon our assuming our responsibility, not avoiding it.

Our ability to incorporate these basics into our every day approach to life is, of course, a matter of faith. Faith is not an end in itself, it must always have an object. In this instance, it is faith in the revealed plan and character of God.

Occasionally when we ask couples to trust God in one of these areas they act as though we were asking them to take some great leap in the dark. Faith is not a leap in the dark, it is stepping out on reasonable assumptions which we can see from our perspective are firmly rooted in fact. When we are out driving, few of us timidly slow down as we crest a hill in order to make sure there is a road on the other side of the crest. We have faith that the road engineers would have placed any number of warnings if there was anything to fear. Thousands drink soft drinks straight from the can without ever once peering into the can to make sure there isn't a dead mouse in it. They are exercising faith.

We have managed to manufacture a fair amount of controversy over certain parts of the Bible, but the basic principles governing everyday living hardly seem controversial. No denomination was ever the result of an argument as to whether or not one should love one's neighbour, or if God has plans for Christians to develop the character of Christ. Everyone who recites the Lord's prayer, if they think about it, recognises our need to forgive as we are forgiven. For most, these very basic principles are considered above interpretation. Accepting them is no problem, provided one has no problem accepting the Bible.

For most of us this is the point of faith, because when we say we have faith in God we mean the God of the Bible. Faith in the Bible as the inerrant word of God is not a leap in the dark. Personally, I believe there is as sound a basis for assuming that the Bible is accurate as there is for assuming I have at least one functioning kidney.

For many, this type of confidence has been undermined by misguided theologians who infer that one must commit intellectual suicide to accept the Scriptures as a source of fact. This, in turn, has the effect of placing belief in the Bible in the leap-in-the-dark category. Nothing could be further from the truth!

The fact is the intellectual case for accepting the Bible stands head and shoulders above the hypothetical theories of worldly theologians.

The reason many don't hear this is that churchmen who deny the basic tenets of the faith will always receive more press attention than those who produce reams of well debated and documented intellectual evidence substantiating the Bible's claim to be the word of God.

We usually direct people with doubts to a small book by Josh McDowell entitled *More Than A Carpenter* (Kingsway) because it gives a good overview of the intellectual stand for accepting the Scriptures.

C.S. Lewis defines faith as 'the art of holding on to things our reason has once accepted in spite of our changing moods'.[2] These basics are the very things we need to be holding on to. They are the foundation which supports the framework of more specific principles required in every day life. We need to see stress as a warning light that we are probably losing our grip on (or at least our awareness of) the character and plan of God. Contrary to some popular opinion, knowledge is a factor in faith. When one considers it is our faith that allows us to stand under pressure, then it is crucial that those factors which form the basis of our faith be near the surface of our understanding.

NOTES

1. Donald MacLeod, in a paper delivered April 1987 to a Rutherford House Conference on AIDS.
2. C.S. Lewis, *Mere Christianity*, Fount Paperbacks, 21st impression, Dec. 1985 page 121.

FACTS AND ACTION

GET FIT AND STAY FIT

Faith is important, but not necessarily mysterious. One of the first steps of faith is good stewardship of the things God has entrusted to us—in this case our bodies.

Studies have shown that those who are physically fit are less vulnerable to pressure and less likely to suffer from stress.

* EXERCISE—The best tranquilliser
If healthy, start slowly, work up to 30–40 minutes' brisk exercise 3-4 times every week. You should get a little out of breath when exercising. If in doubt, consult your doctor first.

* WATCH WEIGHT
A strategy is better than a diet. If overweight, lose a little slowly by EATING LESS.

* EAT WISELY
Avoid sweet things, added salt. Eat LESS fat, especially animal fat, LESS dairy foods, MORE fish, chicken, vegetables, fruit, bran.

* ALCOHOL
A little—at times of relaxation—may be good.
Beware addiction!

* SMOKING
DON'T. Seek help in stopping.

* CHECK UPS
Blood pressure, cervical smears and mammogram (breast screen), if possible check cholesterol level.

I get enough proper exercise   yes–no
    If no—what do you intend to do?

I am overweight   yes–no
    If yes—what do you intend to do?

My diet is healthy   yes—no
   If no—what do you intend to do?

I drink too much alcohol   yes—no
   If yes—what do you intend to do?

I smoke   yes—no
   If yes—what do you intend to do?

I should be having a health check up   yes—no
   If yes—what do you intend to do?

ADOPT A HEALTHY LIFESTYLE

A healthy lifestyle will help you to withstand pressure and PRE-
VENT YOU FROM DEVELOPING STRESS

GET ENOUGH
   Sleep—average 8 hours
   Rest and Relaxation
   Holiday
   Music, Reading, Poetry, Painting, Art

USE TIME EFFICIENTLY
   Discontinue low priority activities
   Delegate wherever possible
   Do things more efficiently

PLAN YOUR TIME
   Have time for the IMPORTANT not just the URGENT
   Decide priorities
   Do things one at a time

LIVE ONE DAY AT A TIME

1. I get enough—sleep   yes—no
                rest and relaxation   yes—no
                holiday   yes—no
                time for music, reading etc. yes—no

Where NO—what do you intend to do?

2. I use my time efficiently   yes–no

If NO—what do you intend to do?

3. I plan my time well   yes–no

If NO—what do you intend to do?

4. I live one day at a time   yes–no

If NO—what do you intend to do?

5

Objective Love

God's agenda is to develop the character of Christ in each of us. The fact that he is love should tell us *love* is the central factor in all that he will be accomplishing in our lives. It is therefore necessary that we allow no ambiguity to surround this word as we go on to more specific applications of love in part three of this book.

There is a line about love in the musical *South Pacific* which goes 'Who can explain it, who can tell you why? Fools give you reasons, wise men never try.' To them love is pure emotion. Dr Ed Wheat, author of *Love Life For Every Married Couple* says, 'Love is an art to be learned and a discipline to be maintained.'

The message that has been coming across for years from song writers is that love is a mystery. But Ed Wheat claims, 'Love is always doing the best for the object of one's love...and there is nothing mysterious about that.' He even says, 'Real love is always a choice backed up by action.'

Why is Ed Wheat so out of step with the rest of the world? Because he is a committed Christian writer who derives his authority from the Bible. By the way, he is not some kill-joy who doesn't believe in romance—he actually specialises in restoring it. He is concerned with exactly the same desirable feelings as the song writers, but he is approaching the subject from a totally different world view.

Depending on the value system underlying one's thinking there can be radical variations in the approach to a given issue. Considering a concept like love in a society with a low estimate of marriage, it is not surprising that Christians have a radically different view. One shouldn't be too shocked at the distorted basics in the front of the last chapter; they are the natural progression of secular thought.

A society which functions under the concept that there is no God eventually must come to grips with the fact that it has no basis for moral or ethical absolutes—no right or wrong.

This means, for instance, that laws are no longer made on the basis of right and wrong, but rather 'acceptable or unacceptable'. We don't have a law against murder because it is actually morally wrong to kill another human being, but because it is socially unacceptable (unless the victim is yet unborn).

With no moral or ethical absolutes we have no solid basis for addressing issues of character. For example my selfishness can't be challenged as wrong until someone's civil rights are violated. And even then it is not character which is being called into account but rather a cause-and-effect pattern of behaviour.

This inability to speak in terms of character has had the effect of forcing psychologists and sociologists to address relationship problems in terms of technique. This technical approach fits in very conveniently with the mind-set of the age where we seem to think that technology has an answer to every problem. 'We have the technology'—and yet we still have no answers to the problems of divorce, suicide or drugs, to name a few.

God's goal for every believer is that we develop the character of Christ. By this standard we have an extreme character deficiency. The primary character quality emphasised in the Bible is love. The quality of love commanded by God is one which requires us to invest our resources in the wellbeing of another—the exact opposite of selfishness. We definitely have a problem, because selfishness is our most dependable human characteristic and it is 180° from God's requirements.

Society doesn't officially recognise the problem, basically because it doesn't recognise any authority beyond its own consensus to censure any particular character quality. In a secular society selfishness is not so much a problem as it is a right! I have a right to be selfish. I have a right to do my own thing. I have a right to look out for old number one. The standard question is: 'If I don't look out for myself, who will?' Certainly the average citizen recognises there is some sort of a problem when he sees beer cans and Kentucky Fried Chicken wrappers on the pavement ten feet from a litter bin.

The way in which we view love and selfishness is the major distinction between a Christian philosophy of life and a secular philosophy of life. Secular society recognises the basic selfishness in all of us as normal human nature. Christianity sees selfishness as the major manifestation of our fallen nature.

Our decision as to whether selfishness is a right or a problem will determine the direction in which we will move in many other decisions.

This is a watershed issue, crucial to our faith, central to marriage and critical in our response to the pressures of life. If our understanding of love is as pivotal to our response to life as the Bible indicates then certainly it is foundational to any strategy in dealing with stress.

This battle against our selfishness is certainly the central issue of our entire journey towards maturity in Christ. Probably the central scripture on this topic is Matthew 22:36-40 ' "Teacher, which is the greatest commandment in the Law?" Jesus replied: " 'Love the Lord your God with all your heart and with all your soul and with all your mind.' This is the first and greatest commandment. And the second is like it: 'Love your neighbour as yourself.' All the Law and the Prophets hang on these two commandments." '

The significance of this passage can't be over stated. 'All the Law and the Prophets hang on these two commandments.' This is the Lord of Glory, who is also called the Word, saying that the primary message of the Word is—a love relationship with God and a love relationship with our neighbour. This means that love is the 'bottom line' of what Christianity is really all about.

It is also significant that this passage comes from what could be seen as a stressful situation. The Sadducees had just had a go at trying to embarrass Jesus and now the Pharisees had him on the spot. However, it was this pressurised situation that afforded the opportunity to express one of his most crucial teachings. A modern context may have found Jesus saying 'I'm glad you asked that,' illustrating that pressure has the potential for both stress and greatness.

Brian, the fellow in chapter one with the 1934 MG, and his wife Dorothy discovered just this. They weren't applying their faith to their marriage. They had been the willing victims of their own selfishness. She had her ideas of enjoyment and he had his. Brian kept saying 'I can't see why all the fuss. Can't a couple simply work, eat and sleep and relax a bit at their hobbies?' It wasn't until he realised that marriage is more than single life with domestic and sexual services thrown in, but total commitment to another person, that things began to change. He realised that he had been giving a 1934 MG roadster a higher priority than his wife.

Renewed commitment to their marriage did not mean simply developing increased tolerance to a substandard condition, it meant working on their relationship. They both had to learn a more objective form of love. She had to develop a genuine interest in his projects and find ways to be of use when possible. And he had to invest less time in his own projects and search out the positive side of some of the things she wanted to do.

One of the problems of a marriage which reaches this state is partners become too absorbed in their own self-interest to allow sufficient time for communication. Consequently they are not always sure of what it would take to please their partner. This same preoccupation with doing their own thing has also meant there has been no opportunity to blend their tastes. There may be a few women who would be immediately and intrinsically motivated to restore a vintage roadster, but most of those who would eventually enjoy such a project would do so only after being 'sold' on the merits by a loving husband who wanted to 'broaden her cultural horizons'. And the same is true for Dorothy's chances of getting him interested in the flower shows which she enjoys.

One of the hallmarks of a secular society is defining love in such a way as to shift the emphasis from commitment to emotion and desire.

This has resulted in millions of couples entering into divorce proceedings saying 'The love has gone out of our marriage.' They had lost 'that old feeling'.

Eros love which motivates romance and the sexual dimension of marriage is fuelled to a large extent by emotions and desires. Phileo love, which is the friendship dimension of our marriage, looks for certain desirable traits in the one being loved. However, agape love, the type which God is demanding, requires nothing from the object of that love. It is motivated by pure commitment.

In one sense 'I love you' is a declaration of taste. 'You have what it takes to attract and hold me.' It is flattering to hear someone say 'I love you,' because it implies we are desirable, but it can be pretty precarious, because we know there are times when we are not desirable. 'I will love you' is a statement of commitment. We don't say 'I will love you,' but it is important to know that our partner's 'I love you' is backed up by 'I will love you.' Part of our problem may be the fact that we like to hear and say 'I love you' as an affirmation so much that the implied 'I will love you' is forgotten. Or maybe we never knew it was supposed to be there in the first place.

Marriage is largely a friendship/partnership, but the distinguishing mark of this friendship is romance. This is the only friendship where 'the two become one flesh'. Consequently eros romance and phileo friendship are both integral components of a successful marriage.

Eros love is the special finial at the top of this relationship that sets it apart. As such, it is totally dependent on the friendship for its very existence. Romance is the first casualty when the friendship is in troubled waters.

Romance is supported by friendship but what supports friendship? Logical question—the answer is commitment. This is where agape love is indispensable.

Romantic love involves someone who looks, smells and feels so special that they 'turn us on'. Friendship relies on common interests, goals, tastes, etc, but commitment relies on our ability to overcome what is probably our most basic instinct—selfishness. We probably made the commitment based on the other factors, but humanly speaking it is extremely exhausting to maintain commitment once those factors seem to evaporate.

Agape love has the necessary commitment to go nose to nose with our basic selfishness and win every time. In one sense agape love is simply a quality of behaviour demanded by God. It is also the quality of love to which God is committed and therefore any commitment on our part to love in this way automatically receives God's energy to assure we are not overcome by exhaustion.

This issue doesn't come into focus any more clearly than in marriage. Tom and Alison told us that it had been over a year since they had sexual relations. Alison was so completely put off by the idea that she couldn't even tolerate the slightest physical contact. Tom realised that this required patience on his part, but wondered just how long he was required to be patient.

Considering what we said earlier about romance being supported by a friendship,we spent just enough time to establish that there were no actual sexual factors contributing to this. We then went straight on to question them regarding the friendship of their fourteen-year marriage.

We found that they began their marriage with very little in common. They were both committed Christians. They were both involved in leading their church's youth work and both used the New International Version of the Bible. The idea of exploring mutual interests, tastes, and backgrounds hadn't crossed their minds. The ensuing years had been filled with professional pursuits, raising children, and when opportunity permitted individual hobbies.

There were several factors involved in restoring the romance lost through years of living cheek by jowl without the friendship to support such intimacy, but the main thing was a commitment to build the friendship. Each human being is a unique collection of weird and wonderful characteristics and although the person we marry has some matching characteristics they are only a small percentage of the whole. Therefore, it is extremely important that we are sure of sufficient common ground to contain the stretching and growth that God intended when he brought such diverse individuals together.

In teaching marriage preparation we tell those who would be involved in this important ministry that if they don't ensure that the engaged couple have identified the common ground in their relationship, some marriage counsellor will have to do so later. This is exactly what was involved here. One thing they had in common was a strong commitment to biblical Christianity, which is why they sought help rather than a lawyer. Pulling things back together takes work and self-sacrifice.

The paradox of life is that happiness cannot be attained by directly seeking it. It is only when we are actively concerned with the happiness of another that we find real happiness.

A good deal of the time this is painless, frequently it is great fun, but we must recognise there is more than one side to love. Probably the most unattractive term in the Christian vocabulary is self-sacrifice. It sounds all at once colourless, boring, painful, uncomfortable, and the absolute antithesis of happiness. It is so diametrically opposed to the spirit of the age which pollutes our every breath, that even Christians avoid using the term. I certainly don't enjoy using the term because I fear that it will erect mental barriers before I am completely heard out.

I suppose we could talk about the principle of love; that is what it amounts to. Love definitely invests in the welfare of another and because it is the antithesis of self-interest, it does so with no thought of return. But there is a sense in

which the word 'love' is too positive to convey sufficiently
the idea of the cost involved.

I am talking about the principle represented in:

> Greater love has no-one than this, that one lay down his life
> for his friends (Jn 15:13).
>
> For whoever wants to save his life will lose it, but whoever
> loses his life for me will find it (Matt 16:25).
>
> Nobody should seek his own good, but the good of others (1
> Cor 10:24).
>
> Each of you should look not only to your own interests, but
> also to the interests of others (Phil 2:4).

*These scriptures claim more for love than simply doing good
for one's neighbour. They proclaim love as a direct attack on
our self-interest. It is exactly this dynamic which brings life to
any facet of any relationship.*

Carol is an example of this. Her relationship with her
husband Ted had grown cold and was fast becoming frigid.
Not only was he not the sweet fun-loving man she had
married, he had developed several unacceptable characteristics and habits as well. He drank too much, he per-
petually smelled like a cigar, he didn't talk enough and
when he did it was always critical of her and the children.
At one time he attended church, but now his Sunday mornings were reserved for golf. Carol knew that the fact that he
spent less and less time at home should bother her but given
the state of their relationship it was a relief. This made her
feel guilty.

When a friend gave her a book on marriage she read it,
hoping to gain some insight on how to wake Ted out of his
oblivion. She hadn't read too far when she decided that the
book was unrealistic and therefore not worth her time. The
author was saying that if she wanted anything to happen in
her marriage, she would have to assume responsibility to
make it happen. The unrealistic part was the fact that
everyone knew how hard she had already tried and how
insensitive Ted was.

The really irritating part was that the author had defined love as total giving of one's self and then implied that failure in love was failure as a Christian. Didn't he know that one could give too much? When she heard the same thing in a sermon she asked her pastor if he had read the same book. He said no and reminded her of the scriptures he had used. Carol broke down. She realised the Holy Spirit was giving her a message loud and clear that she had an investment to make in Ted.

When she discussed this with a close girlfriend, mentioning Ted's critical spirit, the girlfriend suggested that she also had a critical spirit. The friend suggested that she list all of Ted's positive qualities. Carol thought she could probably do that on the back of a matchbox, but by this time she was too ashamed to say so. She got quite a shock when she reached thirty-six without too much effort.

She then committed herself to finding at least two things to compliment him on each day. She made it her business to find out what he was involved with each day. She put a lot of extra thought into meals and her personal appearance. Shortly after she began this campaign her next door neighbour told her that she needed her head examined. Her words cast some doubt on the wisdom of pouring all that energy into a sick marriage with a totally ungrateful man. Fortunately Carol had already seen that Ted was not totally ungrateful. She also remembered she had really committed herself to this action to please the Lord, not just Ted and certainly not her next door neighbour whose marriage didn't speak too highly of her understanding of marriage.

She persevered and things began to really change, but surprisingly enough Ted hadn't changed all that much. He did cut down on the cigars and made an effort not to smell like one. At first Carol thought he had changed considerably but then she realised that she had changed more. She was now seeing him as someone she loved. She had actually fallen in love with him all over again. In fact she took up golf in order to be able to spend more time with him. She actually began it on Sunday mornings when she would far rather have been in church. However, that didn't last too long. Once he realised how much fun they were having together, he was willing to play golf on Saturdays and take her to church on Sundays.

One might say that Carol began enjoying life more once she committed herself to making Ted's life more enjoyable. Matthew 6:21 says 'For where your treasure is, there your heart will be also.' Faithfulness in the kind of love which invests in the well being of another will not remain an effort or a duty indefinitely. It will soon be characterised by affinity and desire.

Like the rest of God's commands, the call to this quality of love is not an arbitrary condition to demonstrate allegiance to God. It is based on a very practical principle which is vital to bringing relationships through troubled waters. It would seem that God puts forth the more crucial parts of his teaching in the form of commands but still desires that we will identify the principles such as Matthew 6:21. Obedience to God has its own rewards, generally in the form of changes in ourselves.

When our actions are designed to bring about change in our partner they are not love or obedience, they are simply manipulation.

Some issues such as love are so basic that a bit of lateral thinking is required to bring in a new focus. Rather than ask 'How can I be more loving?' more insight is gained through identifying areas where we have allowed ourselves to become a bit too selfish. We are such undoubtedly selfish creatures living in a self-serving world, but once we recognise this we can use the negative patterns of our own self-interest to identify specific areas where we can be more loving.

In a lot of instances this will take divine insight: we will have to ask God to show us just how selfish we are by pointing out specific issues. This is not dangerous introspection, it is a commitment to change. Husbands probably have a bit more opportunity to demonstrate consideration. For the most part wives feel personally responsible for the overall tidiness of the house. This means every way we use the house brings an opportunity to demonstrate love or selfishness. Soiled clothes can be left lying around or placed in the dirty clothes' bin; books, magazines and personal belongings can be put away or allowed to clutter. Wiping down the kitchen counter after making a snack, clearing the table and the occasional use of a loo brush, are all things that someone has to do. It would seem logical for these things to be dealt with by the person who makes the mess.

Some of these things are educational in nature, we just never think of them—although it would seem that a reasonably intelligent man would suspect that his dirty socks do not have the strength to march off to the dirty clothes' bin on their own, regardless of how strong they may smell. It took me a time to convince Joyce that she shouldn't rake the leaves from her flower beds onto my lawn because it filled the lawn with rocks that I had to rake back off to avoid ruining the lawn mower. But it didn't take her as long to come to grips with that one as it took her to get me 'house trained'.

Taking the most comfortable chair, the choicest piece of meat or assuming everyone else wants to view our favourite TV show, are fairly obvious manifestations of our selfishness. There is always a dilemma as to whether to make these decisions in favour of ourselves or others.

Selfishness is definitely related to our survival instinct, but the insidious thing about it is we want to survive better than others.

This is why it affects the way we function in relationships.

If we have been really decimated in the past, our survival instinct may work overtime. We think it unwise to make ourselves really vulnerable—we might get hurt. We basically say 'I'll give you anything I have but I won't give you me.' Oh, we will give ourselves in the form of time, which is a sacrifice, and our money which represents our time, but we won't allow others close enough to the real us to inflict any pain.

When we think of selfishness, most of us think of the biggest piece of pie and the most comfortable chair, and we consider that to be inconsiderate if not sinful. However, when we begin talking about self-preservation in various forms, we are not so quick to call that sin. After all, there has to be some survival instinct!

Turning the other cheek may be a Christian response but what if the other guy is using brass knuckles? Should a wife allow herself to be beaten? We certainly believe in survival and we are sure it is a God given instinct. We are not talking here about protecting ourselves from grievous bodily harm, but a lack of vulnerability which works against a meaningful relationship.

Self-preservation becomes a relationship problem when we allow our fear of being hurt to get in the way of our ability to love.

We won't reach out in a genuine way because to do so requires a vulnerability greater than we are willing to risk. We won't give ourselves in a relationship because it could prove uncomfortable and possibly extremely painful, so we settle for arm's-length relationships with all around us. This is more believable at the office or church but it is difficult to imagine how one could live with, sleep with and propagate with another person without the necessary vulnerability. Propagation certainly does require vulnerability, but only physical, not necessarily psychological.

We do know of marriage partners who are starved of physical affection. Sexual relations have not occurred for months or years, and many would be pleased if they could receive a good cuddle without sex. However, many more couples feel the effects of psychological distance. Their partner will make love (if you can call it that) but won't let them know their thoughts. Some have even learned to fake psychological intimacy in the same way some wives have learned to fake an orgasm to avoid worrying their partners. All of this is done in the name of self-preservation, to avoid being hurt. Unfortunately the pain is not actually being avoided, it is being diverted to our partner. The cautious one may not feel the pain but their partner feels the pain of rejection because of the barriers erected.

The fact is the pain we fear is actually hypothetical. The pain that we suffered in the past may have been real enough and perhaps it was deliberately inflicted, but there is absolutely no reason to assume future relationships will bring similar pain. Another fact is that pain has a purpose. We can't always identify that purpose but the fact that God is love and he is sovereign rightfully brings us to the conclusion that it is not without purpose. Ed Wheat speaks of this pain: 'If you are afraid to try because you are afraid you will be hurt, consider this: the risk of pain is always the price of life.'

This type of fear is a common barrier to real self-surrendering love, but there is a way through it. First Corinthians speaks of faith, hope and love and it states that the greatest is love. The reason for this is that love is the result of faith based on hope.

The Bible recognises that love doesn't always come naturally and isn't always easy, which means it will sometimes require faith. A sovereign God has given us his propositional truth in verbalised form in our language. This is our source of hope. Romans 15:4 'For everything that was written in the past was written to teach us, so that through endurance and the encouragement of the Scriptures we might have hope.' And of course the Bible's definition of faith includes 'being sure of what we hoped for'.

Everything...was written that we might have hope. God's word contains his purpose, his plan, what pleases him and what makes him weep, as well as the way he has historically responded to men and women in various situations. We have documented evidence of the heart, mind and character of God. This is the hope we can be sure of and therefore step out in faith. Faith is not a leap in the dark. Far from it, it is based on logical propositions.

The message is this, the main thing that pleases the Lord and that he requires of us is love. We know two things about this love. Firstly it is not subjective, focused on the way we feel about a person. It is an objective investment in their well being. It is much more than a technique, like the smile of the personnel director telling you why the company will no longer be requiring your services. It is a heart attitude. Secondly, we know this quality of love is possible. God would not require something of us that was beyond our ability, at least not beyond the ability he is willing to provide. We also know that he is love and therefore he would not require us to make ourselves vulnerable to any pain that would be useless.

In the next part of this book we will be exploring some of the major issues producing pressure in marriage. We won't be attempting exhaustive coverage of each topic, but we will be covering the major pressure points. We will also be giving God's ways to deal with the problems. Some of these could be taken as gimmicks or formulas, but any effort to make theological truths cogent and practical will be seen by some as a gimmick. Keeping it in the context of the character and plan of God identifies these distillations of biblical truth as 'hand holds' on what might otherwise be a slippery issue. The fact that a large suitcase may be easier to carry because of its handle doesn't necessarily make the task easy. The hand holds we are providing don't make seemingly impossible tasks easy but for many they are crucial in bringing them into the realm of possibility.

FACTS AND ACTION

WHAT TYPE OF PERSON ARE YOU?

Casual about appointments	1 2 3 4 5 6 7	Never late
Not competitive	1 2 3 4 5 6 7	Very competitive
Good listener	1 2 3 4 5 6 7	Anticipate what others are going to say (nod, attempt to finish for them)
Never feel rushed (even under pressure)	1 2 3 4 5 6 7	Always rushed
Can wait patiently	1 2 3 4 5 6 7	Impatient while waiting

Take things one at a time	1 2 3 4 5 6 7	Try to do many things at once, thinking about what to do next
Care about satisfying yourself no matter what others may think	1 2 3 4 5 6 7	Want good job recognised by others
Slow doing things	1 2 3 4 5 6 7	Fast doing things
Easy going	1 2 3 4 5 6 7	Hard driving
Express feelings	1 2 3 4 5 6 7	Hide feelings
Many outside interests	1 2 3 4 5 6 7	Few interests outside work/home
Unambitious	1 2 3 4 5 6 7	Ambitious
Casual	1 2 3 4 5 6 7	Eager to get things done

High scores mean you have Type A behaviour

Low scores mean you have Type B behaviour

Some Type As are known as the AHA Types—Angry, Hostile, Aggressive

Type As live in the fast lane, often workaholics, welcome change and are almost addicted to stress and 'adrenalin'

Type Bs are more laid back, more philosophical

TYPE As—AFTER PROLONGED, OFTEN SELF-IMPOSED PRESSURES AND STRESSORS, MAY DEVELOP HIGH BLOOD PRESSURE, HEART ATTACKS, STROKES

TYPES

I am a Type A   yes-no

If Yes, study and apply the following hints.

Hints for Type As:

—Slow down
—Accept what you cannot change
—Smile
—Listen more, talk less
—Do one thing at a time
—Enjoy delays:—read

—listen to music
—enjoy the scenery
—switch off
—Do not take on more than you can handle
—LEARN TO RELAX

One can take positive steps such as:

'Progressive relaxation' where groups of muscles are tensed and then allowed to relax.

Adopting good posture helps relaxation.

Massage from a qualified practitioner, but gentle stroking from wife/husband is relaxing.

Scripture memory and meditation is very relaxing and accomplishes the additional objectives of gaining wisdom and insight.

Other techniques are available from qualified and responsible teachers—preferably under medical supervision.

Great care should be taken because many relaxation techniques on offer in the secular world are derived from Eastern religious practices and the occult.

The type of person we are influences the way in which we respond to life and therefore the way we respond to people. This in turn affects our ability to love. The good news is we can change, we do not have to be prisoners of our temperament. We can actually make our temperaments work for us rather than against us and our loved ones. The 'SALT' exercise at the end of the next chapter may add some practical insight.

Part Three

GOD'S SPECIFIC STRESS PREVENTION IN MARRIAGE

6

Forgiveness Is An Act Of Love

First Peter 4:8 tells us 'Love covers over a multitude of sins,' which underlines the fact that forgiveness is a natural and necessary function of love. It presupposes that loving means we automatically 'make allowances' and forgive because to love someone brings with it the desire to see them in the best possible light. An unforgiving, bitter spirit will scarcely allow us to see or believe anything but the worst about a person we are out of sorts with—the worst possible environment for love. Failure to forgive is the most potent source of self-induced stress for the individual and we can imagine no greater source of pressure on a marriage relationship.

Love requires vulnerability and forgiveness is making oneself vulnerable. There is sometimes a sense of security in holding on to an offence as if it protected us from a repeat performance from our partner. Failure to forgive usually results in holding the offence over our partner as if they were on probation. Forgiveness makes us vulnerable because it usually means inviting one who has hurt us into a full and unrestricted relationship with no probation. This means giving up the safe ground upon which we feel more secure, which goes against our self-preserving instinct.

Undoubtedly, the most classical association of love and forgiveness is the fact that God so loved the world that he gave his Son as a basis for forgiveness. The God who hates sin loves sinners. His righteousness would not allow him simply to forgive our sin and restore the relationship. He had to separate the sin from the sinner before he could enter into a relationship with us. Roy Hession states: 'To create, God had but to speak, and it was done. But to redeem, he had to bleed.'[1] Having separated us from our sin he destroyed it. Forgiveness separates the sin from the sinner in that it makes a distinction between the person and their actions. It allows us to affirm the person without affirming their wrong doing.

One Sunday morning, after I had spoken on forgiveness, a couple came to me in a very critical mood, asking if forgiveness didn't tend to condone sinful behaviour. I had already been warned that there were a few from a fellowship that had been split over a scandal among the leadership—these two were still smarting. They were concerned that forgiveness to some in their fellowship meant ignoring the events which had occurred and thereby approving of sinful behaviour.

Forgiveness is not an approval of sin; quite the opposite, it is a recognition of sin as sin, otherwise forgiveness would not be required. One cannot say, 'I forgive you,' without also implying that the other person is guilty, just as a request for forgiveness is an admission of guilt.

Offences can be overlooked and forgiven simultaneously and frequently this is the right approach, but forgiving and overlooking are not synonymous. Sins which have extensive repercussions often involve discipline, restitution or both. A child can be made to forfeit a certain amount of his spending money to pay for a broken window while experiencing genuine forgiveness. The fact that discipline or restitution are involved need not interfere with forgiveness, and forgiveness need not affect discipline and restitution.

Occasionally actions need to be taken to assure that our forgiveness is not confused with approval. Parents of a child living with a lover may not feel free to visit the home where the couple are living together but still do everything in their power to project love and forgiveness. The parents avoid those things which endorse sinful practice but do whatever possible to endorse the people. Forgiveness is an approval of the person; it says 'You are too important to me to allow an offence to come between us.' It is the separation of the sin from the sinner.

Holding on to resentment is a major stress producing factor in marriage. It is often times that which makes us feel like there is a wall between us. Resentment hinders our communication, our desire to pray together and our willingness for love making. Resentment is the great spoiler of life.

We don't always recognise its harmful effects on our mind and emotions until there's a real build up. Resentment can start small and accumulate.

'I wish he'd call when he's coming home late.'

'You'd think she could remember to put fuel in the car when she uses it.'

'I wish I got as much attention as his computer games.'

'She makes me feel she's comparing my earning power with her brother.'

When we don't forgive on a daily basis these negative thoughts begin to add up and the resulting resentment we feel towards our partner shows itself in negative thoughts which produce negative emotions and finally actions.

Unforgiveness brings stress into the marriage even when it's not between partners. When I hold an unforgiving spirit against my parents, in-laws, children, boss or someone down at church—it affects my relationship with the Lord and how I relate to others. If my partner forgives the offending party there is a good possibility my vendetta will be against my partner as well (if only subconsciously) because I'll feel she's not being loyal to me.

Forgiveness isn't always easy; in fact, sometimes it seems impossible, but the more we understand about it the greater our ability to apply it. Jesus said the truth would set us free. The following isn't intended to sound like 'The Four Spiritual Laws of Forgiveness' but it is a means of providing 'hand holds' to climb out of the pit of bitterness.

1. FORGIVENESS IS MANDATORY

There are two things that God demands of Christians in no uncertain terms—loving and forgiving one's neighbour. Nonetheless, we always manage to get the shoe on the other foot and think someone should pin a medal on us whenever we manage to meet either of these requirements.

Forgiveness is mandatory, it is a non-optional principle of life. God's forgiveness has one condition to it. It is very black and white. In Matthew 6:14,15 it says, 'If you forgive men when they sin against you, your heavenly Father will forgive you. But if you do not forgive men their sins your Father will not forgive your sins.' There is nothing ambiguous about that. We pray quite frequently, 'Forgive us our sins as we forgive those who sin against us.' It is a proportional thing. One woman we were working with had been carrying an offence against her husband for some time. When we reminded her of the Lord's prayer she said 'I know. I just don't say that part.' She knew it would be very dangerous. This goes on to amplify the next point.

2. UNFORGIVENESS IS EXPENSIVE

Bitterness costs—spiritually, psychologically and physically. *Spiritually* it costs us our fellowship with God. We cannot say, 'You and I are all right, Lord—it's just that woman you gave me,' or 'It's the rest of this lot that I'm bitter with. You and I are fine, Lord,' because we are immediately cut off from God. An attitude which breaks fellowship with our partner automatically breaks fellowship with God. This is undoubtedly the case because withholding forgiveness is, when you think of it, one of the most self-centred acts we can enter into. Unforgiveness is fuelled by self-centredness which is the opposite of love. Unforgiveness blocks love. Spiritually it is costly. It costs us our fellowship with God.

Psychologically it is costly because we are in bondage to the person we won't forgive (not always our partner). They are not in bondage to us; they may have forgotten all about the incident and be totally unaware that we are still stewing over it. We are actually reliving the offence as if to make sure we keep the wounds open. In fact, this is a recipe for extracting the maximum amount of pain from a given offence when forgiveness would remove the traumatic issue from our life.

Physically it is costly. Long before the present pre-occupation with stress, people such as Dr S. I. McMillen[2] were listing physical maladies that were commonly associated with bitterness. Their list is almost a duplicate of the common physical disorders associated with stress for the simple reason that bitterness is a stress inducing agent. Momentary bitterness toward another driver or long term resentment both contribute to our overall stress level. The offence is the pressure. An offence not forgiven is pressure mishandled and pressure mishandled produces stress. Hence, unforgiveness produces stress.

3. GOD IS IN CONTROL

He is sovereign.

> The Lord Almighty has purposed and who can thwart him? His hand is stretched out, and who can turn it back? (Is 14:27).

In other words, God is powerful. He has a plan and the power to see that his plan is implemented.

As stated in chapter four, the plan is that we develop the character of Christ. The fact that God is sovereign makes it logical to consider offences as somehow fitting in with his plan. Is there a lesson in this? Asking, 'What are you trying to teach me, Lord?' recognises the sovereignty of God. 'Why me, Lord?' is asking God if he was out to lunch when this painful incident occurred.

Given that God is sovereign, some logical questions might be, 'Where was God when a child was molested?' 'Where was God when a woman was raped?' 'Where was

God when there was an unnecessary killing?' The answer is, God was there. The real question is why he allows those things to happen. The quickest and most intelligent answer is, I don't know. However, I do know that if I accept the Bible as the final authority on his character, then I must accept it as the authority when trials come. I must trust what he has revealed about himself in his word rather than my current experience. Because I have learned that experience can lead me astray.

The daughter of a lovely Christian couple that we have known for over twenty years was murdered. Her boyfriend threw her out of a third storey window. They had a lot to come to grips with. This couple who are fairly well recognised Christians in their community were suddenly faced with a choice. They could forgive this young man or they could allow bitterness to neutralise completely everything God was doing in and through their lives.

The trial came up some time later and quite naturally the press found it interesting how they were responding. They foresaw this and prepared a statement which contained the line, 'We are struggling to apply our Christian faith to forgive this young man who has so drastically altered the course of our lives.'

How these things fit into God's plan is not always immediately visible. But no longer can anyone look at them when they try to console their loss of a child and say, 'But you don't understand,' because they do. They paid the price to join a very exclusive club; one they did not want to join because the dues were too high, but they are members.

Difficult times are, almost by definition, a test of our faith. Do we actually believe the things which, at better times, we claim God has revealed about himself? The world is looking on to see if Christianity actually does make a difference, or whether Christians are trapped in the same psychological mire as the rest of society.

Many will remember what has probably been the most effective sermon of the 80s which consisted of a very short statement by Gordon Wilson of Enniskillen forgiving the IRA bombers who had just killed his daughter.

Remembrance Sunday fell on the eighth of November in 1987. A constant drizzle fell on the town of Enniskillen as a small band of pipers accompanied the Ulster Defence Regiment, police and firemen in a march to honour the glorious dead of Royal Enniskillen Dragoons and the Royal Enniskillen Fusiliers.

At 10:45 am thirty pounds of explosive were detonated by the IRA, collapsing the community centre on some eighty people gathered to watch the parade. Among them were Gordon Wilson and his twenty-year-old daughter Marie, a student nurse. Gordon survived but Marie was one of the eleven who died as a result of that blast.

You may recall the minute but remarkable interview of Gordon Wilson that was relayed around the world because of its content. 'My wife Joan and I do not bear any grudges. I am sorry for those who did this, but I bear them no ill will. I prayed for them last night... may God forgive them.'

The immediate repercussions of those words were far greater than the news interest they generated. Normally such an incident sparks off a series of retaliatory sectarian killings, but Gordon's words caused those who would normally have led in retaliation to hold their wrath out of respect for Gordon Wilson and the daughter he had lost.

The long range results are the fact that God in his sovereignty has allowed this family to play a staring role in demonstrating to the world that people walking with God can forgive what seems to be the unforgiveable. Gordon has a firm grasp on the basics. He said 'We see it as God's plan, even though we might not understand.' Along with Job, he recognises that nothing happens that is not allowed by God, for a purpose. Like Job, he also has his critics. We were recently told that some have accused him of giving aid and comfort to the IRA because of his stand.

In a letter approximately two and a half years after the disaster Gordon told us their mourning has brought them into some pretty dark patches. They aren't without pain. Gordon still claims no further insight into God's reasons and states that he has no official or specific ministry. However, it is well known that he expends a fair amount of energy on a 'ministry' of reconciliation between the Protestant and Catholic communities. And when he speaks people listen. God has provided him with the credentials.

4. FORGIVENESS IS AN ACT OF THE WILL

Forgiveness is a decision not to hold something against our partner and a commitment not to bring the offence up again.

Often we confuse forgiving and forgetting. We get this idea because God says, 'I will remember their sins no more.' But I think we have to analyse this. Is the God who knows everything about anything in the universe ignorant about something that I know? God forgave my sins yesterday and I still remember them but does he not remember them any more? Obviously that is a Hebrew hyperbole, meaning that he does not hold our sin against us any more.

In large corporations it is not possible to sack an employee simply because they deserve to be sacked. There must be proper documentation. Problem employees are given letters of counselling which are filed in an Unfavourable Information Folder. Then if enough information is amassed, they can be sacked without the union going on strike.

When God forgives us he tears up our Unfavourable Information Folder. He is not ignorant of it but he does not have it on file against us any longer. When we need to forgive someone else we know we cannot just forget it. There is no such thing as selective amnesia. However, we can certainly say that this is not on file against them anymore. We can tear up the Unfavourable Information Folder.

Unfortunately, many couples find a measure of security in retaining such files. There is a sense in which possessing some bit of unfavourable information about our partner provides a 'hold' over them. This is the dynamic of blackmail. It is using past mistakes as a means of manipulating each other. That is a fairly straight forward case of self-interest.

With some individuals, feelings of insecurity seem to be the motive for holding on to resentment. Their hurt has added to their insecurity, but they view holding on to the resentment as a form of insurance against further hurt, at least from the same source. We have several close acquaintances who handle their relationships in this way.

To one degree or another, we all have times when we respond to an offence with resentment. Sometimes we actually 'project' an atmosphere of resentment. Very insecure individuals tend to do this as a matter of routine. It is as if they had an aerosol that could spray a protective shield of resentment around themselves. This atmosphere is to ensure others make no demands on them because they have been sinned against and the offending party is kept on his or her best behaviour.

Resentment is also a source of comfort when we feel insecure because it provides a way of retaining proof that others also sin. If we can find flaws in those who are admired then we have less to be dissatisfied with in ourselves. Resentment then becomes a handy way of ensuring that others don't demand too much of us while we demand more of them, at the same time convincing ourselves that we aren't as bad as we thought we were.

The sad thing about all of this is the fact that it adds to our original insecurity. This 'protective atmosphere' which was designed to hold others at arm's length works so well that they can't get in to love us either. Love is the very thing that would add to our security.

When we are aware that we are using this shield of resentment we must remind ourselves that we are viewing the situation from our limited perspective. We are using our own devices to protect ourselves rather than to depend on the God who is in control.

We claim to believe God is love, that he has a plan for our lives and that he is in control, but the minute we feel insecure we tend to trust in ourselves rather than in him.

And to top it all off we use our lack of faith in these other areas as an excuse to slip out of our responsibility to forgive.

There are a few things which will make this decision to forgive easier.

We can identify the specific things that are causing bitterness, pain, and making life miserable. It is possible to lose sight of the specific offence and to develop a 'free floating bitterness' which is difficult to deal with because forgiveness is very specific. It would be helpful to list these items causing bitterness.

We can analyse each item on our list for lessons. 'What were you trying to teach me in this Lord?' God is sovereign. The offending party may well be a tool in God's hand to get our attention about a particular problem we are having. If someone implied that we were insensitive it may be that God is using that person to make us aware that sensitivity is something we need to work on. This can be true even though their statement may be inaccurate. The Bible records several instances where God allowed the evil intentions of men to be used in bringing about good. It is easier to forgive when we focus on the possibility of positive consequences.

We can list the problem areas that God is dealing with in our life. This should help to put the offences from the above list in perspective. People who have difficulty forgiving, frequently have difficulty recognising their own short comings. They may dismiss them quickly or justify them, but at any rate they see little relation between their own transgressions and the offences committed against them.

This was the problem experienced by Rob and Doreen mentioned in the first chapter—working through to forgiveness was far from automatic. He was full of joy because Jesus had taken *all* his guilt, including the adultery. She, on the other hand, was stewing in bitterness. It wasn't until she finally understood what sin really was that the parable of the unforgiving servant (Matt 18:21–35) actually began to sink in. She could see why Rob needed salvation: after all, he was a documented adulterer, but she had never done any such thing. When she finally did come through, recognising that sin was sin regardless of its form, she re-invited Christ into her life on the basis of her new understanding that she was indeed a card-carrying sinner. Coming to grips with her own sin and experiencing the forgiveness of God in her own life Doreen was then able to forgive Rob. The pressure was lifted, the stress disappeared and their sex life blossomed to the point where a sex therapist was the last thing they needed.

Then, by an act of the will and verbally, forgive the other person or persons. It may be inappropriate actually to verbalise forgiveness to the offending party but it is still good to speak those words aloud for God and ourselves to hear. Make a commitment never to bring this up against them again. Try to remember this person without remembering the act. It's not going to happen all the time; we may have to hark back to that original commitment and say 'I've made a commitment not to bring this up any more.' The important thing is continually to enforce that commitment as long as there is any residue of resentment. Be sure to tear up any lists that have been made. When we truly do forgive it takes the sting out of remembering.

We can find ways of demonstrating our new attitude— anything to let this person know that we love them and that we have forgiven them. This is important because there are some situations where it is not possible actually to speak forgiveness directly to the individual. For instance it may not be wise to say 'I forgive you for being so patronising to me.' That may seem to be more of an accusation than a forgiveness.

Stress is not caused by someone else's sin, but by our own. The original offence is the pressure. If unforgiveness is our response then stress is the result of that decision.

Life is not ruined by the sins committed against us, only by the way we respond to those sins.

NOTES

1. *We Would See Jesus*, CLC, 1958, page 13
2. *None Of These Diseases*, Marshall Pickering

FACTS AND ACTION

OTHER TYPES OF STRESS

Some cancers are more common in those *who bottle up emotions* and in people who often *feel hopeless and helpless*.

Some other effects of stress are more common in those who *do not forgive and bear resentment* and in those who are often *lonely*.

I need to open up my emotions   yes–no
I may have deep hidden emotions   yes–no

If yes to either: Honesty with yourself is important and a willingness to open up, even if it could apparently make you more vulnerable.

However, you may need help from a trusted friend or from a reputable and trained counsellor to help you uncover the emotions and express them.

I need to feel less hopeless and helpless   yes–no

If yes—have you been able to think through why you feel like this? You may need help to discover the source of these feelings and deal with them.

I need to forgive   yes–no

If yes—what do you intend to do?

a) The only person you harm by bearing resentment is yourself. It continues to weaken your ability to deal with pressures. The subject of your resentment may be unaware of it and is probably not affected by it.

b) People often want to wait till they feel like forgiving, but a first step often needs to be an action: a meeting, a letter, a handshake, an arm round the shoulder, a demonstration of forgiving. The feelings will follow.

FORGIVENESS IS AN ACT OF LOVE 103

TYPE A

While good to change behaviour, it is more important to change whole attitude to life

The meek shall inherit the earth—not TYPE As

What is the point of a dead Type A?

If you believe that God is in charge of everything then there is only so much you can do. Leave the rest to him.

OTHER TYPES

a) Emotions should not be suppressed. They should be admitted to God and then help requested to express them where relevant and without hurting others. If hidden, God should be asked to reveal them, so that they can be exposed and dealt with.

b) Hopeless and helpless feelings should never exist when you remember that God is on the throne; that he has you in the hollow of his hand.

c) Forgiveness is a must, otherwise we will not be forgiven. Do not wait for feelings—act and speak. God will provide the feelings in time.

d) Loneliness is never necessary. We should be surrounded by love and care in the church. But even where that fails Jesus is always there with us and IN us.

7

Honest, Vulnerable Communication

Communication has been called the life blood of a relationship and that is certainly true. Just as blood carries oxygen and nutrients to individual cells, communication is the vehicle of relationship. It is the transport between two minds and the prime ingredient of *the two becoming one*.

Because no relationship can exist without communication, many consider lack of communication to be the primary reason why relationships break down. That is a fallacy of logic. It is true that failure to communicate is almost always involved in relationship breakdown, but it is only the instrument of breakdown and not the cause. Communication is a technical skill and as such is only a tool which can be employed in building or destroying a relationship. The primary cause of breakdown is much deeper. It is a matter of self-interest gaining the upper hand.

It is important to make this distinction because the history of mankind is speckled with people blaming tools and instruments for failures which were actually failures of character. None the less communication is an extremely important element of a relationship and deserves considerable attention. The way forward through a relationship barrier is to pick up the tools of communication and bore on through. The most fool-proof way to keep the selfishness of one from alarming the survival instinct of another into a state of irrevocable panic is to communicate.

Communication is the primary weapon in our fight

against marriage breakdown. However, superior weapons have never been as decisive a factor in the outcome of a battle as the determination with which they were used. One does not have to be a great communicator as long as he or she is committed to communicating. Failure to communicate is to surrender one's marriage to the adversary. It is he who is our real enemy, not our partner.

Communication is not something which will just happen; it is the result of a decision. We can sit preoccupied with our own thoughts or fantasies, engulfed in TV, buried in a book, engrossed in a hobby—or we can communicate. We may feel like prisoners of war, fettered by fear, in bondage to bitterness, arrested by aggravation or detained in depression, but freedom almost always involves a decision to communicate.

People who are non-talkers must decide to communicate, but then so must compulsive talkers, because not all talking is communication. The fact that a person cannot stand silence does not make them any more a communicator than a person of few words.

This is because a decision to communicate is more than a decision to open one's mouth. It is a decision to understand and to make oneself understood.

It is a decision to transmit an idea, concept or just plain information to the understanding of another. Opening our mouth is often an important part of the process but it is only effective after we have determined our objective.

There are four main communication objectives involved in preventing the build up of tension in a relationship: informing, demonstrating respect and appreciation, blending tastes, and resolving differences. It is not possible to place these in a hierarchy of significance, any more than most mechanics could say which is the most important tool in their kit. They may be able to tell you which one they use the most, but would quickly add that they wouldn't want to be without their least used tools.

1. INFORMING

Ignorance not only breeds fear, it also breeds rejection.

A partner who isn't kept informed feels shut out of the relationship.

This is especially true if others have been made aware of information that they haven't. Keeping our partner informed of what we are thinking and how we are feeling about events is the most effective way of avoiding problems. It is also the most basic level of demonstrating respect.

However, this objective of keeping our partner informed is more than simply passing along news bulletins. It is to know and to be known. The depth of our relationship is determined by the depth to which we know one another, which is, in turn, determined by the level of information offered. This is a decision, a decision which will usually be the result of a battle. The battle is between love and selfishness and it is conducted in the mind and heart of each partner.

There isn't always a battle. Sometimes love is in complete control of the field and is able to provide safe passage for the information. On the other hand, when self-preservation has the upper hand information is as severely censored as a Soviet newscast before Glasnost.

There are no battles fought when selfishness has been in control for so long that there is no one around who can remember any such vulnerability as Glasnost. The only thing in living memory is the censored news bulletin. 'Please pass the salt,' is not the type of information deep relationships are made of and yet self-preservation often so subtly anaesthetises our longing for deep love that censored news bulletins become our only form of communication.

Saying there is no memory of vulnerability might tempt some to say that isn't because selfishness is in control, but because ignorance is. It is kinder to think of ourselves or others as failing due to ignorance rather than selfishness, but it is not very realistic. There is a sense in which inconsiderateness is ignorance but it is ignorance born of selfishness—'Don't want to know.'

2. DEMONSTRATING RESPECT AND APPRECIATION

For most of us the primary evidence that we are loved is the fact that we feel respected and appreciated. If we don't feel respected as a human being and appreciated for who we are, we have a hard time believing we are loved. Failure to feel loved doesn't automatically add up to feeling rejected, but it is very nearly so when this lack of respect and appreciation involves someone quite close. When we feel rejected we automatically make the assessment: 'This person is not an effective part of my support system.' Living with a marriage partner or family member that we have no confidence would be supportive in times of trials is a tension in and of itself.

It should be obvious that demonstrating respect and appreciation belongs in the front line of defence against stress in marriage and family life. Unfortunately it is not all that obvious to many. Most of us recognise our own longings for respect and appreciation, but many are oblivious to these longings in others due to a mixture of ignorance and self-centredness.

On the issue of ignorance, there are two questions that always go through my mind: 'Isn't he or she aware of my respect and appreciation?' and 'Is my opinion all that important in the first place?' On the first, even if they *are* aware, they still find reassurances quite comforting. On the second, I may not feel important and therefore not attach much weight to my opinion, but it is important, if for no other reason than the fact that I am their husband, father, son-in-law or whatever. It is always valuable to have the respect and appreciation of those close to us.

Gary Smalley likes to use the word 'honour'. He claims 'Honour is an attitude that someone is valuable.' In his book *Love is a Decision* he says: 'When we honour someone, we make a decision that a person is special and important. Biblically (and thankfully), honour was not always something that had to be earned. It was given as an act of grace to someone who didn't deserve it.' He goes on to say: ' "Honour" doesn't cast pearls before swine—but neither does it mean that you treat a person like a swine until he measures up to your standards.' Honour or respect is certainly the most effective lubricant against friction in the home and it is counterproductive to withhold it in hopes of changing another person's behaviour.

There are times when I want to engage in conversation but can't seem to think of a topic or any information that needs to be passed along. More often than not this occurs on a car journey to or from a speaking engagement. I realise that one of the reasons that I have the desire to converse when I have nothing pressing to say is because I want to let Joyce know I appreciate her. Since I finally figured that one out I simply begin by saying 'I was just thinking how fortunate I am to have you for a partner,' or we comment on a job well done or our appreciation of special thoughtfulness. There are a lot of ways to communicate 'I love you.' It might be said that the best stress prevention in marriage is simply demonstrating respect and appreciation.

3. BLENDING TASTES

This is a part of developing oneness. The Concise Oxford dictionary defines 'blending' using such terms as 'mingle intimately' and 'harmonious compound'. Effective communication does intimately mingle the ideas and attitudes which go into developing our tastes. This makes it possible to develop a harmonious compound which will keep down the cost of the relationship. Every relationship has its cost, and that cost shows in areas of differing tastes. If she likes to play golf and he doesn't there is a price to be paid. Aside from a certain amount of time a couple agrees to spend apart, either he pays the price by indulging in a game that doesn't really bless him, or she pays the price through abstaining from something she really enjoys.

But with a bit of dedicated communication there is a better than average chance that they will be able to blend their different tastes. If he is approaching the game from a truly open minded position she may be able to persuade him of the merits of the game. They may find an alternative game that they both enjoy. She could come to the conclusion that this particular game has become a dominating force in her life, and that relationships, this relationship in particular, are worth much more. Some people have developed interests as a substitute for relationships and giving up such obsessions is not so much a cost, as it is an emancipation.

4. RESOLVING DIFFERENCES

This is more than matters of taste. For the most part it is addressing matters of ethics and values or at least procedures which seem to convey ethics and values. The word *seem* is critical here, because things are not always what they seem. This is where communication is essential. We are frequently offended by a mannerism of someone close to us because we read too much into it. The problem is, most of us find it easier to overlook what we consider offensive behaviour than to address it. Consequently we are never able to distinguish between an act that is inconsiderate and a misunderstanding of a given situation.

A lot of our early misunderstandings have their roots in family background. Her dad always helped clear the table after the evening meal, his dad retired into the lounge to read the paper. Chances are, clearing the table will not automatically become established routine for a young man whose father wasn't in the habit of doing so. This is not necessarily chauvinistic or lazy. Clearing the table and sharing the washing up is an ideal way for a couple to spend time together, but not everything can be done together. A man who seizes the opportunity to read the paper while dishes are being done may be the pinnacle of sensitivity and actually spend quite a bit of time with his wife, while the guy who clears the table may also be clearing out for an evening with the boys. But any wife who is offended by her husband's lack of support in this area, has the responsibility to raise the issue for discussion rather than sending out a barrage of non-verbal signals.

One of the most common sources of pressure in marriage is the failure to confront one's partner when things are going wrong.

We don't like what we see, but we feel that addressing the situation will bring more hassle than the original problem.

Tom and Alison, the couple we mentioned in chapter five, Objective Love, who were attempting to build their friendship, had this problem. They were both sure that the other could not cope with discussing problem issues. They seemed to believe the worst about each other. The relationship was pockmarked with rows over the usual disagreements, finances, disciplining the children, and where to spend the holidays, etc. The rows were the direct result of 'sweeping their differences under the carpet' rather than make any attempt to resolve them. This failure to address issues as they arose resulted in a mild form of 'free floating bitterness' which had no actual focal point. Even issues which had been settled were continually regurgitated because of this attitude. In any marriage this will result in a lack of respect, believing the worst and a total lack of oneness between partners.

If this is to be avoided problem issues must be confronted. Proverbs 19:11 says 'A man's wisdom gives him patience; it is to his glory to overlook an offence.' However, we generally over rate our ability to 'overlook an offence'. Indeed there are times when we shouldn't. There are certainly times when it is our duty to challenge particular behaviour. If we fail to do so the result is an attitude problem.

There are two tests for issues which may require confrontation: is this detrimental to the relationship and is it detrimental to my partner?

This means that I actually have to confront myself first.

> Why is this behaviour or situation bothering me?
> Is my perception warped, bent, slanted or biased?
> Am I hypersensitive, insecure or paranoid?
> Or narrow-minded, short-sighted, prejudiced or even bigoted?
> Could it be that I am opinionative, hypercritical, or fussy?
> Am I being doctrinaire, dogmatic, pedantic or snobbish; over zealous, fanatical or perfectionistic?
> Am I being just plain selfish?

The issue may be detrimental to the relationship because it makes it extremely difficult for us to respond correctly to our partner. This is actually our problem and needs to be stated as such. This particular practice may be detrimental to my partner because it shows a lack of Christian character in my partner and is thereby detrimental to her maturity. It may be both. Adultery would be both: it would make it hard to respond lovingly to our partner and would also be selfishness on the part of our partner.

Confrontations made just because we are fed up with something are usually the result of failure to analyse the problem or letting oneself off lightly. Confrontations based solely on being 'fed-up' are comfort oriented. Not that we should never make them but we must recognise them for what they are. 'Dear, could you please stop making that noise?' is typical.

It is important that we don't overwork 'comfort oriented' confrontations and try never to allow our own comfort to be the motivation on more critical issues. It usually takes a bit of praying through to arrive at the right state of mind and heart so that we can share out of concern rather than self-interest.

Joyce and I certainly had problems in this area. I wasn't backward about letting my displeasure be known, but Joyce wasn't very assertive. We didn't understand the need for proper confrontation, much less the subtleties of motives just discussed. Joyce's reluctance to confront me was compounded by the fact that listening with an open mind was something I hadn't discovered yet. In addition, I was better with words and if that failed my natural stubborn forcefulness would get my own way.

That is a sure-fire combination for developing pressure in a marriage. One partner is frustrated by never being able to share ideas about critical situations. The other partner knows, at least deep down inside, that they are treating their partner unfairly, and that there is a problem that they are not addressing to the best of their ability. They are both under pressure and possibly suffering stress. This is exactly where the marketing couple, Don and Sharon, were in chapter one, and still are along with thousands of others. Sharon was frustrated because she felt Don was deliberately keeping her in the dark on several decisions. She felt he was doing so because he knew his choices could not stand the least amount of logical scrutiny. Fortunately for us, Joyce had what it takes to hang in there until I grew up—which was quite some time. We only hope Sharon is that tenacious. Many are not.

The purpose of these last three paragraphs is to challenge 'winners'. If you have had a pretty good track record at winning arguments or having your ideas implemented (a nice way of saying 'having your own way') you need to ask yourself some questions.

- Do you have superior verbal skills?
- Are you generally more forceful?
- Do you use 'emotional blackmail' to manipulate your partner?
- Husbands, do you rely on your position as head of the house to gain the co-operation of your wife?
- When she disagrees, do you see that as being unsubmissive?
- Would your partner say decision making is a joint venture in your marriage?
- Are there any topics of discussion which are forbidden in your marriage?
- Is there any topic that you deliberately avoid?

- Are you easy to talk to when the topic is controversial?
- Do you have the courage to ask your partner what he/she thinks of your answers to these questions, and then listen openmindedly to the answers?
- Remember, fools don't lose arguments. They never recognise when they are wrong.

Blow-ups can be avoided through thoughtful wording. Hundreds of couples have thanked us for the little phrase we teach on our marriage weekends, 'I have a problem I think you can help me with.' It is effective because it doesn't put your partner on the defensive.

Another key consideration is to speak in terms of actions rather than character. This separates the sin from the sinner. Hearing a parliamentary debate one wonders how the words 'British' and 'reserve' were ever linked together, because it sounds like a free-for-all. But they do have some rules. One may say: 'The right honourable gentleman has misled the house,' but not, 'The right honourable gentleman is a liar.' Every family could well afford to adopt this rule. Rather than call her husband a slob the frustrated wife could say: 'The right honourable gentleman has left the bathroom looking as if it had been used to degrease a tractor engine.'

A person might easily be forgiven for thinking that the Christian approach to dealing with conflict is simply to yield when it can't be avoided all together. However, Matthew 18:15 tells us, 'If your brother sins against you, go and show him his fault,' which means we must do something about our differences. Confrontation can be an act of love. Conversely standing by allowing our partner to develop bad character qualities, simply to avoid the hassle, is the antithesis of love. We have seen people turn into 'monsters', or at least develop some monster-like qualities simply because their marriage partner was afraid to challenge them. Selfish character traits that go unchecked by loving concern don't take long to crystalise into hideous defects.

We might also be forgiven if we considered compromise appropriate. It may seem like a play on words, but conflicts should be resolved, not compromised. Compromise focuses on what I want out of the agreement, while resolution has the best interests of the relationship at heart. Setting out to resolve conflicts and differences is looking for a way we can both be winners; compromising is settling for two half winners.

There are times when a form of compromise may serve as a practical first step toward resolving a difference or blending tastes. Roger and Mary had a real problem that was threatening their marriage. Roger was extremely conservative in everything he had ever done. He had been to public school and university and was a conservative evangelical Anglican—with emphasis on the Anglican. This suited Mary right down to the ground until she attended a women's meeting and received the baptism of the Holy Spirit. She began by visiting a local house church and by the time we talked to them, Roger felt they had completely taken over her mind. In fact, he felt she needed to be 'deprogrammed' as if she had been brainwashed by a cult.

With all due respects to the house church movement, this particular house church did seem a bit heavy handed with its authority; and with respects to the Anglican church, even Roger had to admit his was a bit more dead than alive. He had attended her church on several occasions but just couldn't stick it, and she wouldn't leave her church to go back to their parish church. They knew this was threatening their marriage but felt helpless to do anything about it. It became clear that it wasn't so much a matter of their unwillingness to give up their respective churches as their inability to stick their partner's church. What they needed to do was to go hunting for a church in which they would both feel comfortable. This was a tough assignment and it obviously had to be a compromise. But, they finally did find one where they could both worship and begin to work on oneness of spirit.

The road to resolving differences must sometimes begin with compromise, but a compromise ceases to be compromise if and when we learn to be genuinely happy in the altered situation. This can only happen if we enter into the situation with a genuinely open mind focused on the relationship rather than our own desires. This often requires a lot of soul searching and prayer, especially when it means leaving behind comfortable structures such as liturgy, and entering into something that is so unstructured as to appear to be chaos.

It is exciting when both partners know the other is not comfortable with the new situation, but is praying to grow to relax and to be comfortable with it, and both see that effort as a tremendous affirmation. 'My partner is willing to make a lot of uncomfortable adjustments just to strengthen the relationship with me. This gives me the strength to make sacrifices for my partner.'

Another consideration in resolving such differences harks back to the fact that God is sovereign. He was in control when we got married and there is a good chance that being forced to look for the positive points in a situation we haven't really liked may be a real blessing.

There are many specific issues which place a marriage under pressure. Many of them are not directly problems with the marriage relationship itself but are inextricably linked to it. Infertility, for instance, is such an issue. It seldom has anything to do with the state of the marriage, but it can affect the relationship. Such a problem requires understanding beyond relationship wisdom. But it does require communication, especially if we want to keep this from affecting the relationship. Good communication assures that we, together, are fighting the problem rather than allowing the problem to divide us and have us fighting each other.

Some may think it's splitting hairs to say raising children is not a marriage issue, it is a family issue. And yet, most would agree that it is possible to do a good job of one and a bad job of the other. Any couple who are going to raise children should read several good Christian books on the subject, but even more importantly, they need to communicate in order to function as one. Anyone who doesn't believe we are born with a fallen nature has failed to observe the natural instinct that all children seem to have for playing one parent against another. Although parenting is somewhat distinct from the primary marriage relationship, a strong and effective marriage is a crucial element in effective parenting. And it is effective communication which will keep problems in parenting from becoming marriage problems.

One of the main parenting issues to cause marriage problems is the disciplining of children. A couple may begin with agreed objectives and policies to reach them, only to come unstuck over enforcing their rules. They have agreed that the children should have their beds made before they go off in the morning or they are restricted after school. Dad comes home to find the kids playing out of doors and their beds unmade, or through a slip of the lip he discovers Mother made their beds. He goes ballistic, calling her totally irresponsible and deceptive. He accuses her of trying to win the favour of the children at his expense. 'You always look all soft and loving which makes me look like a big green meany for sticking to the rules,' he says. She then fires back a few choice words about his being authoritarian, autocratic, cold, insensitive and unloving.

Of course, it's obvious they are breaking just about every possible relationship principle. It begins because of his frustration due to not being in control of the situation. He leaves for work two hours before the children leave for school, so he must rely on his wife to see that the rules are followed. They are both aware that he sees this particular issue as being more critical than she does. There are any number of possible extenuating circumstances that would have formed very valid reasons for not applying the rule that day. However, he made the most common and fatal error: he believed the worst. He accused her of attempting to undermine both his authority and his credibility. Instead of addressing the action, he made accusations about her character and motives. Rather than return good for evil she felt it would be in her best interest to return evil for evil.

Returning good for evil breaks the cycle. Returning evil for evil completes it and assures that all the barriers are up.

Meaningful communication is almost impossible at this

point. For Christians, learning communication skills consists mainly of identifying areas where our selfishness can quite easily gain the upper hand. Concern over the development and discipline of our children can hardly be selfish, but an obsession with our own ideas is. It is this obsession which makes us poor listeners, oblivious to the feelings of others and oblivious even to the facts.

We need to learn to communicate effectively when things are going well, because once a problem begins, communication is difficult even for those who are quite skilled. For this reason couples need to make a covenant with each other to communicate, regardless of how difficult things become. Once evil has been returned for evil, about the only words which can precipitate meaningful dialogue are something in the order of: 'I was wrong about (and name the offence). Will you forgive me?'

One important area of preventing stress through communication frequently overlooked is communicating with God—not just presenting him with our problems but listening for answers. When we earnestly discuss a matter with God it eases the pressure. This is equally true as a couple. Regular times of prayer as a couple reinforce our awareness that Jesus is the third partner in the relationship. As we come into his presence we become more aware of his sovereignty and frequently find specific wisdom and insight to deal with the situation.

When our youngest son was sixteen he ran away from home and was gone for six weeks. We were sick with worry, because he was going through a bad patch, experimenting with drugs and a poor choice of friends. We didn't know what might befall him. Joyce spent several entire days in prayer for him until she felt she had the assurance from God that he would alert her to pray any time Bill was in danger. This allowed us both to relax, knowing God would notify us when our concern was necessary, which he did do a few times. Other than that, we had a supernatural peace.

This is undoubtedly the most important communication, because our relationship with God is the highest priority relationship we have. This means that prayer is more than a religious ritual to be entered into by schedule, and it is not an emergency procedure. It is communicating with a friend who also happens to have both the wisdom and power to solve the problem. However, as with any other relationship it requires more communication than a quick, panicked 'What do I do now?' This doesn't honour the relationship which is basic to all other relationships, as we will see in the next chapter.

8

Protective Priorities

We cannot go through life without pressure, but some pressures can be avoided. Time management courses promise to deliver us from the tyranny of the urgent through effective planning and scheduling. This is definitely one very useful tool in stress prevention. It circumvents some of the avoidable pressures. However, time management courses only provide the tools to honour our priorities. Priorities not commensurate with our world view are an open door to stress.

A great deal of pressure comes from emotionally charged decisions involving our commitment to various relationships. Pressure from this quarter is involved in many marriage problems, particularly among committed Christians. We are told to consider others more important than ourselves...love our enemies...love our neighbour ...love one another...husbands love your wives... honour your father and mother. The last two clash frequently enough to keep quite a few marriage counsellors busy.

Melvin and Deloris seemed a typical middle-aged couple. Melvin was a banker who from all outward appearances was a very caring person—always ensuring that people had the things they required. Deloris had a slightly different perspective. He was caring, but much more so to his very demanding mother than to her. Deloris also had reason to believe that her mother-in-law resented her and that the mother-in-law deliberately engineered situations which would demonstrate the favouritism that she demanded. As far as Deloris was concerned Melvin could always be counted on to side with his mother against her when the chips were down.

Melvin didn't want it to be this way but he had two problems: he was weak willed and he had no structure for dealing with such dilemmas. However the solution to the problem lay with him. He finally grasped the structure provided by the Bible and claimed the power of the Holy Spirit to apply it. He came to grips with the full meaning of 'leaving and cleaving'. He realised it meant that his obligation to honour his mother was not meant to encroach upon his relationship with his wife and daughters. He also realised that if God had provided a framework of priorities, then he would provide the strength to stick to it when unreasonable demands were being made.

We serve a sovereign God whose plan for life enables us to develop a few simple guidelines which cut through this kind of emotional dilemma. The Bible doesn't give us any charts such as the one below. However, it never uses the word 'trinity' either, but because it tells us that there is only one God and that the Father, the Son and the Holy Spirit are equally God, we understand that God is what we call the Trinity. This chart is a similar composite of scriptural facts. It begins with the command to 'Love the Lord with all your heart, soul and mind', then it moves on to 'Love your neighbour'. It covers our very closest neighbours, our family, then goes outside the family and on to loving neighbours through more formal ministries.

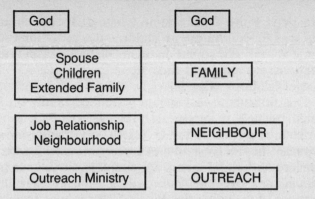

No Christian has a problem understanding that God is his or her number one priority relationship. Life has no real meaning without him. Just as my salvation is based on a personal relationship with Christ, believing he died for me, my daily personal relationship is maintained through communication, prayer and listening for the Lord to speak through his word.

When God said that it wasn't good for Adam to be alone, he created Eve, and thereby the family which would be the basic unit of society and he protected it with a hedge of simple priorities. There was, however, no doubt that the husband-wife relationship was the highest priority human relationship. It is the only one where God ever said 'The two shall become one.' Passages like Ephesians 5:24,25 speak of the commitment involved. 'Now as the church submits to Christ, so also wives should submit to their husbands in everything. Husbands, love your wives, just as Christ loved the church and gave himself up for her.'

No other relationship has such a biblically prescribed level of intimacy, permanency and oneness. There cannot be any doubt that our marriage is our highest priority human relationship.

This commitment provides the best possible environment and model to protect and train up children. The Bible sees this priority as so self-evident as to be naturally observed even by unbelievers. 'If anyone does not provide for his relatives, and especially for his immediate family, he has denied the faith and is worse than an unbeliever' (1 Tim 5:8). Naturally with children this provision calls also for love and direction. 'Fathers, do not exasperate your children; instead, bring them up in the training and instruction of the Lord' (Eph 6:4).

It is difficult to include the extended family on such a chart because it immediately brings to mind honouring parents by not accepting a certain job or ministry calling because they don't agree with it or would miss us. (The concept of 'leaving' limits the amount of influence parents should have over their married children.) That is not the purpose of including this block. It is because many find it easier to minister continually to their neighbour's needs rather than their own parents' or they can write letters to any but their parents.

With regard to loving one's neighbour, there is a distinction between my neighbour who is my employer and my neighbour who just shares my neighbourhood. Firstly, not only is my employer my neighbour, but I am also selling him something and I have a responsibility to make sure that he gets value for money. I am selling him my time. Secondly, occupational relationships are frequently close and represent a great investment in time. To the Christian each relationship is a divine encounter. It doesn't take much imagination to theorise that the depth and consequence of the relationship is somewhat proportionate to the eternal value God intends to accomplish through it. For example, when God chooses to work on us through a relationship he seldom uses casual acquaintances. It is usually a fairly consequential relationship that we have a hard time avoiding.

I believe that it is necessary to make this distinction regarding occupational relationships. Too many Christians have little or no testimony because they are doing exactly the same thing as the world. Basically what it boils down to is being dishonest with their employer—falsifying of records, documenting work that has never been done, spurious expense accounts and time cards are all too common-place.

This chart doesn't imply that my occupation is more important than my next door neighbour. These priorities tell me how I am to *relate* to others. My own needs are nowhere on the chart. The priority is not derived from direct concern for retaining gainful employment, but from the responsibility to deliver the goods that have been promised.

There is a place where these two actually clash with each other, which is why I think a priority distinction needs to be made. While sitting in my office on the job, one of the men from my house group comes in, flops down and says, 'Dave I've got a problem.' He's my neighbour, but right then I'm not being paid to solve spiritual problems. Obviously, anyone can chat for a minute or two to a friend who comes by, but if I am continually seen to be ministering to Christians when I am being paid to administer an office, this certainly damages my credibility and the credibility of the gospel.

My next door neighbour is none the less important. Because we live in town our neighbours are a dentist, a shopkeeper and across the street an inn keeper. There is a sense in which spending time in chit-chat with the shop keeper, inn keeper or dentist simply to build bridges is as spiritual as the marriage counselling we do with hurting couples.

This could seem as though we simply shove people into little boxes in order to facilitate some simplistic, legalistic decision-making process. Not so. There are two things that one must remember in trying to apply any teaching on priorities. Firstly, priorities are not a prison; they cannot be applied legalistically. They serve as a basis for common sense reasoning in decision making, not as a substitute.

Secondly, the factor which precludes the legalistic usage of priorities is urgency. When decisions are being made, consideration must be given as to the urgency of the particular situation. If, just as I am walking out of the house to take my wife to dinner, a couple come who have just had a real knock-down, drag-out fight, and are both in tears, they need immediate help. It's not an abuse of our priorities if we take the time out to help them rather than invest in our own relationship. The priorities are given so that if my wife is in the same emotional state as the couple, I will choose to minister to my wife's needs.

Incidentally, any marriage partner who honestly feels they are their spouse's number one priority is much quicker to recognise such emergencies and to back decisions which may require an unwanted change in plans.

One of the smartest moves we have seen to establish this type of credibility was in some marriage preparation sessions we were conducting for a young couple. Rob and Lindsay were both school teachers. Because he was a PE teacher there was some expectation that he would play team sports on Saturdays—cricket in the summer and hockey in the winter. In fact, he had listed this as one item on a list of twenty expectations we asked them to complete as one part of their marriage preparation. The object of the exercise was to examine each other's lists for compatibility of ideas. Then after lists were exchanged they were to mark each other's expectations to indicate either agreement, difficulty (if they thought that would cause problems), or extreme difficulty.[1]

Lindsay went along with Saturday sports. However, it came out in a subsequent discussion among the four of us that she wasn't actually too pleased with this. He had kept this schedule through university and by Saturday night Rob was usually exhausted. Lindsay wasn't pleased with the prospect of starting off their married life in the same way.

Their church had warned them not to get involved in any ministry for the first year so they would have more time to get to know each other better. She had assumed that Saturday sport was not negotiable. This was her mistake because even if that were true as far as he was concerned, she had a responsibility to voice her misgivings.

As it was, the next week when they came back they told us Rob had decided he would play no team sports for the first year and then they would decide season by season. Smart man. Lindsay has firm, undisputable proof that she is his top human priority. She will most likely give her whole-hearted approval to future seasons, because she knows the decision is being made on how things affect their marriage.

I want to know that in my partner's eyes I come before her hobbies, occupation, ministry and even our children.

God intended me to have that security in my marriage and he also intended that I do all in my ability to convey that same priority to her. When it comes to priorities, probably the biggest pit-fall for Christians is whatever they consider their ministry. It is very easy to confuse teaching Sunday school, counselling or being an ordained minister with our relationship to God. When we do this we automatically place our 'ministry' ahead of our family. I have used inverted commas here because it is not a very exact word. Everything on the chart is a ministry. We minister to God in our devotions and through our awareness of him throughout the day. We minister to our families and neighbours through meeting their needs.

The reason we need to have our priorities correctly aligned is to determine appropriate types of ministry and to ensure that meeting the needs of one doesn't conflict with the needs of another. Loving our neighbour, whether meeting needs through counselling, comforting or hospitality, we need some formula to cut through the emotional red tape involved in conflicting needs.

One simple example of such pressure involved some dear friends of ours. Tom and Alice were both on their second marriage which only had one really threatening flaw. Tom would do anything for his extended family and they knew it. His background taught him that family were never to be let down and it seemed to be scriptural. It also had the unfortunate effect of blurring most of his priority structure, particularly where Alice was concerned. He seemed to operate under the 'blood is thicker than water' principle and she felt very much on the water side. Until they got that straightened out they were under a great deal of pressure any time this issue arose.

Because it sounds 'spiritual' even church attendance gets placed ahead of marriage. Gill's non-Christian husband, Paul, had already left home when we came to speak in their church, but he was very regular about taking their seven-year-old son out for weekends. Gill actually provided accommodation for us that weekend because of having the extra space. We had a fair amount of opportunity to talk with Gill about her priorities over the weekend. She admitted to being at church every time the door was open and came to realise that she had put church activities before her family.

She enjoyed church and thought the Bible could be used as a battering ram to knock down all opposition. When she recognised how far out her priorities were and straightened out a couple of other things in her life, her husband noticed the difference. So great was the change that he was willing to come for marriage counselling. One of his first comments was 'I felt like an unpaid baby sitter.' He moved back in to the house and she still attends church. He hasn't become a Christian yet but he feels he is her top priority next to God, and they have a good marriage.

It was once suggested to me that the Good Samaritan stood out only because he was willing to ignore his priorities when the priest and the Levite weren't. I don't believe the parable of the Good Samaritan is a discussion of priorities but of selfishness. Certain individuals were so focused on their own selfish agendas that they failed to recognise the emergency needs of others.

Church attendance is a priority with us and it is something we look forward to, and all the more so, considering we seldom get to attend our own church. One Sunday morning we received a panic phone call from a young husband who lived near by. He was in tears, at his wits' end, saying they were so far out of their minds that one of them could get killed if something wasn't worked out. I could have said 'Our priority is to attend church. Would you postpone this murder for a few hours?' Obviously I said 'We'll be right over.'

We have tried to help young couples minimise the pressure points and resulting stress that come from over involvement in outside ministry. As a couple marry it is good for them to pray for direction as to how they can serve the Lord together. So often a couple's gifts and abilities complement each other, and they are a stronger force working together. This also helps promote oneness in the spiritual dimension.

Too many couples are involved in different church activities on different nights and are feeling the pressure on their relationship by not having the time to spend with each other and as a family.

We have also had it pointed out that much of the early missionary work would not have been accomplished had the family taken a higher priority than the calling. However, church history and even the Bible itself is pockmarked with incidences of God using people who were unknowingly, and even occasionally knowingly, out of step with God's principles.

The fact that God blesses even at times when his wishes are being ignored is not a case for taking his plan even more lightly—it is grace.

Each generation has had its own unique focus on the Scriptures so that through the power of the revealed word we might address contemporary issues which were not even dreamed of by those actually penning the original lines. This is a part of what makes the Bible contemporary. If there was ever a generation which required guidelines for responsible usage of time it is this one. The fact that the market place is covered with wall-to-wall time management courses is a testimony to the fact that this hasn't gone unnoticed by the business sector. Their biggest problem is that career or money or both has taken the place of God.

This is a logical point at which to consider motives or objectives, because after all, priorities are only a structure to help us reach our objectives. This is why a secular priority structure differs from a godly priority structure. They were designed with different objectives in mind— basically that of serving self or serving others. Hence, one structure places career ahead of family while the other reverses the order.

This is another source of tension—God's people with one agenda living in a secular world which has a totally different agenda. This means that it is very easy to unwittingly adopt structures which are counterproductive in reaching the objectives God has laid out before us. It would seem obvious that the man or woman who says, 'My objective is to please the Lord,' will have different priorities and short term goals from the person who says, 'My objective is to get to the top.' There is nothing wrong with Christians wanting to reach the top, but that must be secondary to pleasing the Lord. When we find we are ineffective as Christians but can't quite figure out why, perhaps it is because we are actually using a structure which is more geared towards reaching the top than pleasing the Lord.

Another factor is that the objectives of the other structures appeal to my fallen nature. I like looking out for myself.

I have found that my motives fall into three major categories: Acquisition, Achievement and Contribution.

My basic greed wants to acquire. My ego wants to achieve. But there is nothing natural in me that really wants to contribute—to invest in the wellbeing of others or to make the world a better place in which to live. It is only the character of Christ forming in me that ever has any genuine interest in that area.

Naturally there is a lot of blurring of motives. I do a lot of soul searching to see if my current contribution is actually the fruit of ulterior motives. Sometimes all three are involved, eg, I feel I have something to say regarding stress in marriage which will be helpful to many couples. I write a book on the topic. I consider this a contribution. However, it would be false modesty to deny that there is somewhat of an achievement factor involved if the job is well done. In addition there are royalties involved which are an acquisition. The question is not whether I feel a sense of achievement over a job well done or appreciate the rather modest sum earned in royalties. The question is: what was my real underlying motive?

Personally, I inventory my motives quite frequently because I don't trust myself. In addition to having a very poor track record where motives are concerned, I don't trust myself because I have seen too many other goal oriented achievers and acquirers who achieved and acquired in the name of contribution. 'I want to reach the top of the ladder to be in a position to offer my family the best.' I know that these motives which are so transparent in others exist in me as well.

I also know I can actually change my motives. This is exactly what is meant by the often glib expression, 'Just turn it all over to the Lord.' If I recognise that my motive is actually to achieve, I can repent of that objective and hand it back to God by thanking him for the privilege of being in partnership with him in making a small contribution towards the kingdom and asking him to provide me with the right heart's desire.

I also know that through changing my objective I can save myself a great deal of stress because I am free from the burden of making sure others recognise my achievement.

Since the main function of Christianity is contribution (as in, 'Love your neighbour') it actually becomes a source of pressure for those who attempt to identify with Christianity and still please themselves. (Hypocrites are always under the pressure of possibly being found out.) This brings us back to the great paradox mentioned in chapter five: 'Happiness does not come from directly seeking it.' Which is why Paul encourages us to 'find out what pleases the Lord' (Eph 5:10).

Pleasing ourselves is stress producing in the long run and pleasing God is stress preventing.

Yes, pleasing the Lord will frequently place us under pressure, but being consistent in it will, in the long run, prevent stress. This is why it is so necessary to identify God's priorities and inventory our motives to ensure that we are making decisions in accordance with our overall objective, to please God, and not simply taking the short sighted course of pleasing ourselves.

NOTE

1. This exercise is found in chapter four of the workbook for engaged couples *Looking Up The Aisle?—A Couple's Guide to Friendship, Romance and Marriage* by Dave and Joyce Ames, Kingsway Publications.

FACTS AND ACTION

DEAL WITH PRESSURES

1. List the main pressures in your life

2. Which of these are self-inflicted or avoidable? (Be honest)

3. Decide what you can do to reduce or discard or deal with any self-inflicted pressures

4. DO IT

5. Analyse each unavoidable pressure. Break each one down into its constituent parts. (Eg if a MAIN PRESSURE is looking after an ageing parent [which is probably unavoidable], what are the specific tasks which cause pressure?)

6. Decide what you can do to reduce any parts of unavoidable pressures.

7. DO IT

A trusted friend may be very useful in helping you decide which pressures are self-inflicted or avoidable. He or she may be able to help you analyse unavoidable pressures, but you may need help from a counsellor to do this.

If you have an outside job there may be specific pressures at work:

—overwork/underwork, pressure on time-deadlines
—when you have or are given aims which conflict with each other
—when you are not sure what your function is and what your limits of responsibility or authority are, or what you will be judged on
—difficult relationships—with boss, colleagues and your staff
—when you are not clear where your career can go or is going
—when you are not always able to be perfectly honest, eg with customers, or with yourself
—office politics
—change of location/home job/responsibilities or increasing travel

—increasing technology
—uncertainty—mergers, takeovers, privatisation, rationalisation, new boss, or threat of redundancy/unemployment
—difficult environment

All of these should be look at as with other pressures

—Which are self-inflicted? Which can be lessened?

The others must be analysed to determine the real causes of pressure and then dealt with where possible. In extreme cases only it may be necessary to change jobs.

9

The Pressures Of Self In Marriage

> For this reason a man will leave his father and mother and be united to his wife, and they will become one flesh (Gen 2:24).

It is not the least bit unreasonable to conclude that oneness at all levels, psychological and spiritual as well as flesh was meant. This is particularly true when one considers it in the light of Jesus' remarks in Matthew 19:6, that husband and wife cannot be separated because 'they are no longer two but one,' not simply one flesh.

God did not include all of the characteristics of himself in Adam that he intended to pass along to mankind. Some of his characteristics were reserved for Eve, eg, God has a mother's heart which he passed along to her. The fact that Eve is referred to as Adam's helper/completer does not mean that Adam wasn't a complete man, and Eve could not have been the effective helper that God intended her to be had she not been a complete woman.

Too many have read the phrase 'The two shall become one,' and superimposed on to it a mathematical, 'Two halves make a whole.' This tends to carry with it the idea that we marry as halves in order to become whole. We are members of a fallen human race and therefore it is not surprising that our partner brings into the marriage certain strengths which tend to balance out our weaknesses. Marriage also brings with it the perspective of the opposite sex, but none of this implies we are incomplete men or women.

Unfortunately, too many of us marry the person we *need* to be complete or we marry the one we believe will meet our needs. Marrying to have one's needs met is something Lawrence Crabb equates to a tick sucking his life sustenance out of a dog, and says too many marriages consist of two ticks and no dog. This is a fertile environment for stress.

Many psychologists, including some noted Christians, claim we have a need for love and a need for significance. Lawrence Crabb, in an attempt to avoid psychological jargon, coined the term *crucial longings* in his book *Inside Out*. He defines crucial longings as '*those desires that must be met if life is to be worth living*'. We have a crucial longing for love and significance.

The fact that the main theme of the New Testament is to love one another and the fact that God has commissioned each believer to a significant ministry, would seem to uphold this. Why else would God commission a bunch of incompetent, grubby Christians of dubious character to go into all the world and make disciples? Why would he take us into partnership saying he had prepared good works in advance for us to do, when he could have contracted out the entire task to a vast company of angels with far more certainty and far more economically? Certainly obeying the command to love and doing the works that he has prepared are a part of God's character development curriculum, but they also fill these crucial longings.

The good news is that these crucial longings are met in Christ. The bad news is that we look everywhere else to have them met.

At first glance, it may seem that a marriage where partners meet each other's basic desires is a very logical and amicable arrangement—'I'll scratch your back and you scratch mine.'

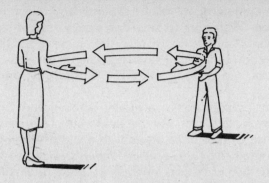

However, when the system breaks down, pressure is introduced into the relationship. The problem comes when our partner, a mere mortal, fails to meet our deep longings. This means that we do not have the emotional capital to meet our partner's longings. For instance, a husband reaches out to meet his wife's longings but she has failed to recognise his attempt. As far as she is concerned her longings are not fulfilled so she doesn't feel she is able to fulfil his deep longings.

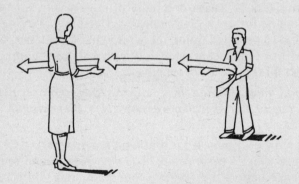

However, when one partner recognises that his or her crucial longing for love and significance is met in Christ, and relies on that fact, they have the emotional capital to meet their partner's longings. The pressure may still exist, but stress is avoided.

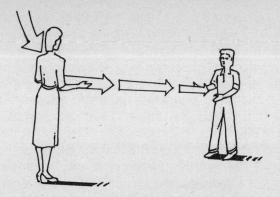

This last illustration is extremely significant because it illustrates one of the central truths of the Christian faith—we can minister on the horizontal, knowing that our sovereign Lord will meet our needs, or fulfil our most crucial longings, in the vertical. We are no longer two-dimensional creatures who can only afford to minister to the needs of those who can return the favour.

Naturally the healthiest marriages are made up of individuals who both recognise who they are in Christ and are not reliant on any other human beings to meet their most crucial longings.

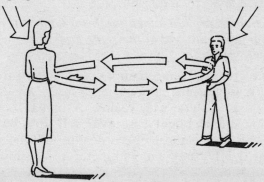

The concept of these illustrations is that our perceived ability to meet the longings of those around us is to some degree related to our awareness that we have had those crucial longings met. Some go so far as to say 'You can't love if you are not loved.' The Bible does not support such a 'Catch 22' concept, but it does tell us that God loves us. This means as far as Christians are concerned, the issue of our resources has been settled. Barbara Streisand sings, 'People who need people are the luckiest people in the world,' but there is a sense in which people who need people are a drain on others. Their wrongly based self-image makes them very demanding as they struggle to have longings fulfilled that were fulfilled at Calvary.

We all have certain insecurities and we don't always respond in a godly manner. None of us is a perfect partner or has a perfect partner. But a wrongly based self-image certainly has great potential for producing stress in a marriage. A wrongly based self-image could very well be a time-bomb waiting for exactly the right conditions to explode. Therefore, even the 'well adjusted' could well afford to take inventory to ensure their confidence is not misplaced.

We were created in the image of God. Therefore, it is necessary to understand certain specifics about God and his plan to have any significant understanding of man. The most significant overall factor is that God did not make man to function apart from himself.

Any attempt to explain man apart from God is like trying to explain a light bulb and at the same time denying the existence of electricity.

An accurate self-image is not possible apart from God. For this reason secular notions of self-image are usually 180 degrees out of phase with reality. A human being apart from God may be bright, assertive, well adjusted and posing what is considered to be a healthy self-image, but it won't be rightly based and will therefore be subject to the whims of fate.

June certainly fitted the above description. She was the PA to the Editorial Director of a large Christian publishing house. She was extremely well respected throughout the industry when she gave up her PA position to start a family. She and her husband Peter were in total agreement that any future employment for June would have to be worked around the needs of the children.

The thing neither had realised was how closely June's self-image was linked to her significance in the publishing world. It is possible to excel as a domestic executive, but it's not such 'heady stuff'. Trading her briefcase for a dustpan was not only less exhilarating, she felt far less qualified. For someone whose self-image is based on 'what I can do' rather than 'who I am in Christ', starting at the bottom presents a problem.

She became very defensive, and read things into every remark Peter would make. He tried to be as supportive as he knew how but even his efforts to help were misinterpreted. Statements such as, 'I'm quite capable,' and 'You don't need to do that,' became common. Peter withdrew in self-defence, which had the effect of assuring June that he didn't love her. Her job wasn't bolstering her ego, her husband wasn't meeting her crucial needs and she wasn't meeting anyone else's. I can't think of a more clear cut illustration of stress induced through a wrongly based self-image.

As Christians our crucial longings are met in Christ and our worth is based on God's standards, but the fact that we live in a world which operates on secular values has its toll on believers. Secular society determines right and wrong on a relative basis, and it assesses the worth of a person in the same way. The besetting sin of Christians is our temptation to borrow from the world's relative values.

We are specifically warned against this. Paul says in 2 Corinthians 10:12 'We do not dare to classify or compare ourselves with some who commend themselves. When they measure themselves by themselves and compare themselves with themselves, they are not wise.'

There are two very good reasons for this. First, we are all unique parts of the body with particular functions and therefore have differing strengths and weaknesses. Second, we have such a limited view of our function in God's overall plan. At best, we are only viewing the underside of the tapestry that God is weaving, which is a very poor view of the overall finished picture.

It is difficult to avoid feeling inferior when faced with others who seem to be so spiritually advanced and still others who are so obviously talented. But we must remember that terms such as inferior and superior are not biblical concepts. God's mind doesn't work that way.

So we know that our behaviour, the rightness or wrongness of our actions, is not measured on a relative basis. We are not condemned by God because we fail to attain the standards of our fellowship and we are not exonerated if we exceed them. Our righteousness is determined by grace according to God's standards.

It is equally obvious that our performance, depending on skills and abilities, is very much a relative thing. There is no spiritualising this. It can often be measured and documented. But still, there is an unknown. We know that many who have demonstrated great skill in communicating the gospel have later fallen into complete disgrace, and we know that there is no immediate measure of the faithfulness of many far less talented. This only leaves us to conclude that it is God alone who assigns the value to our performance. We are convinced that a God who 'makes things that are seen out of things which are not seen' doesn't value performance with a stop watch or a tape measure. He uses the things which are not seen, like the motives, commitment and character behind the performance.

We are convinced that the Bible's term for a healthy self-image is *humility*.

Humility sometimes carries the connotation of inferiority, but that is certainly not a biblical concept. The Lord Jesus was humble and we can't imagine him grovelling in inferiority.

Humility in biblical terms means, first of all, an accurate self-appraisal of the type spoken of in Romans 12:3–8. We are to commit to the Lord the gifts and abilities which surface as the results of such an appraisal, expecting that he will use them in a way which is spiritually significant. 1 Peter

5:6 says 'Humble yourselves, therefore, under God's mighty hand, that he may lift you up in due time.'

Humility is the recognition that anything of significance accomplished by me will not be the result of my abilities, but God's. Jesus set the standard for this humble mind set with statements such as:

> By myself I can do nothing; I judge only as I hear, and my judgment is just, for I seek not to please myself but him who sent me (Jn 5:30).

> For I have come down from heaven not to do my will, but to do the will of him who sent me (Jn 6:38).

> My teaching is not my own. It comes from him who sent me (Jn 7:16).

> He who speaks on his own does so to gain honour for himself, but he who works for the honour of the one who sent him is a man of truth; there is nothing false about him (Jn 7:18).

> When you have lifted up the Son of Man, then you will know who I am and that I do nothing on my own but speak just what the Father has taught me. The one who sent me is with me; he has not left me alone, for I always do what pleases him (Jn 8:28–29).

> For I did not speak of my own accord, but the Father who sent me commanded me what to say and how to say it. I know that his command leads to eternal life. So whatever I say is just what the Father has told me to say (Jn 12:49–50).

It is obvious that if the Lord Jesus could do nothing by himself, then we, by ourselves, can do nothing either. I will grant you that I don't have to be in fellowship with God to paint my house.

I can do a lot of things apart from God. But will they amount to anything? Can I afford to have my self-image based on the things I can do apart from God?

A great portrait artist may think it unnecessary to base his opinion of who he is on God, but who would he be if he were blinded? A great pianist may feel the same, but what would his self-image be if his hands were smashed?

A house painter with God is of greater significance in God's economy than the most accomplished portrait painter without God. The good news is that the real significance of either the house painter or the portrait painter in Christ is not contingent on their skill but on their relationship with Christ. If all we can do is mop floors God still has a significant place in his plan for us, but without him we can do nothing—nothing of significance.

After the resurrection Jesus appeared to the disciples and made it clear why he had taken such great pains to set the example of being dependent on the Father. 'Peace be with you. As the Father has sent me, I am sending you' (Jn 20:21). In other words, he was saying, 'Just as the Father sent me to be a man totally available to all he wanted to do through my humanity, by means of his Spirit, I am now sending you under the same orders. You are to make yourself available to me so I can operate through you by means of my indwelling Holy Spirit.'

By this time, the penny had probably dropped for the disciples, and his words of John 15:5 began to make sense:

> I am the vine; you are the branches. If a man remains in me and I in him, he will bear much fruit; apart from me you can do nothing.

Of course the concept of an indwelling Holy Spirit was totally new, as was the understanding of having an old nature as well as a new nature. Our old nature is at war with God, the new desires to please him, and there is a constant battle going on between the two.

This battle is not without effect on our self-image, regardless of whether one is a first-century apostle or a twentieth-century bank teller. What or who we think we are, our self-image, should, as Christians, be based on what and who we really are. Otherwise we will tend to behave like what we are not. That is, if I believe that the real me is my old nature, I will behave accordingly. I won't think there is much reason to fight the inevitable. However, if I know that I actually am a new creation and the old nature only has power over me when I choose to give it power, I have hope.

Paul gave us hope in this area:

> Now if I do what I do not want to do, it is no longer I who do it, but it is sin living in me that does it (Rom 7:20).

This was not an effort to avoid responsibility but a simple exercise in fixing himself to his rightful identity of hope rather than one of hopelessness.

All this means that the true worth of a person is totally relevant to their commitment to Christ and the purposes of God. The worth of a person is totally contingent on their relationship with him.

Personal worth cannot be found apart from God. Therefore anything which stands in the way of that relationship is counter productive.

David said 'If I had cherished sin in my heart, the Lord would not have listened' (Ps 66:18). The fact that sin cuts our communication with God is reason enough to keep a short account on sin.

> If we confess our sins, he is faithful and just and will forgive us our sins and purify us from all unrighteousness (1 Jn 1:9).

This means all we have to do to be in a right relationship with God is to assume responsibility for our actions—that is what it means to confess. That ensures that the problem of separation from God is dealt with and we can face the world as a child of the King in right relationship. Our self-image is on a right footing.

However, placing this in the context of stress in marriage frequently requires further confession. I may confess to God that the way in which I have been treating my partner is wrong, in which case he will generally reply by telling me to tell my partner. A clear conscience frequently goes beyond my vertical relationship with God. It requires maintenance on the horizontal as well. It means I'll have to use the three most difficult words in the English language—I was wrong. Naturally it would help if I went on to qualify exactly where I went wrong, eg, 'I was wrong in the way I spoke to you, it was disrespectful. Will you forgive me?'

Maintaining a clear conscience between God and myself and between my partner and myself is not only vital to my personal self-image; it is one of the main instruments in building up my partner.

Peter was able to help June immensely once he came to grips with the fact that his self-image depended first and foremost on his relationship with God, and not the rejection June was dishing out. Until Peter came to grips with that there was a sense in which they both functioned as tuning forks. The least tap would send out provocative vibrations lasting for hours. His first step in loving his wife back to normal was simply to absorb quite a few unkind remarks—without flinging them back. Peter was beginning to function much more like a shock absorber than a tuning fork. It wasn't long before June was as well.

It might seem that the price of maintaining a biblical self-image, stepping from self-centredness to God centredness, is very steep. That may be so, but it is good value.

A rightly based self-image makes the difference of whether we function as tuning forks or shock absorbers.

FACTS AND ACTION

BEAT STRESS

SOURCE OF CRUCIAL LONGINGS

Everyone has crucial longings for:
—love and security
—significance or worth or value
When these are threatened, stress may appear.
  People whose basic longings are fulfilled from entirely dependable sources are not vulnerable.

I get my love and security from (draw up an honest list)

_____

_____

I get my significance, worth, value from (draw up an honest list)

_____

_____

All of these sources are *entirely dependable*   yes—no

If NO—what can I do to insure against losing them?

  The Christian view about sources of crucial longings—love, security, significance, worth, value—is that we have been made to be entirely dependent on God.
  The bottom line is that we should get them from him.
  ONLY HE IS ENTIRELY DEPENDABLE. ALL OTHER SOURCES, PEOPLE AND THINGS CAN AND MAY LET US DOWN.
  God may fulfil some of these longings through other people or things and we should accept them and thank him for them without becoming entirely dependent on them.

10

Financial Pressure

The relationship of stress to finance, in common with the rest of these topics, depends a lot on perspective. The Old Testament introduces the concept of wealth as a byproduct of righteousness—but not the reason for it. The modern day gospel of prosperity tends to come across as though riches were a carrot that God dangles before us to motivate us to righteousness.

This seems to be reinforced by passages such as Ecclesiastes 2:26 'To the sinner he gives the task of gathering and storing up wealth to hand it over to the one who pleases God.' The problem is that there is no formula given to ensure one will become the recipient of this reassigned wealth. The subject of this passage is the futility of materialism, not how to gain material possessions.

There is no doubt that the way we handle our finances is critical because in one sense, money represents the distillation of our life's efforts—at least that portion we are willing to sell in the market place. Earning, allocating, spending and saving are equally critical facets of our overall stewardship of life. Mishandling the financial chain at any point brings pressure. This pressure is not limited to the wage earner but is frequently a source of stress throughout the family.

Out of his 168 hours per week a man is willing to sell forty hours to finance not only his remaining 128 hours but also 168 hours for his wife. This is in order to free her to be the full time resident domestic executive and part time paediatric nurse, emergency medical technician, tutor and psychiatrist. He also hopes to finance 168 hours each for his 2.5 children while they are learning to be useful citizens. Obviously, there are many variations on this basic theme which range from being sufficiently well off to avoid selling any time whatsoever, all the way to each family member selling forty plus hours per week.

Why the variation? Some people are able to sell their hours for more than others. Our granddaughter is happy to fold news letters for an extremely modest hourly wage, but some people make literally thousands in an hour. This is a key factor in bringing most of us to the conclusion that it's not so much what one does forty or so hours per week but how much one is able to sell one's time for. This is short sighted but commensurate with our basic selfish nature.

There is a safety valve which will allow us to search the market to get the best price for our efforts without plunging head long into materialism.

> A man can do nothing better than to eat and drink and find satisfaction in his work. This too, I see, is from the hand of God, for without him, who can eat or find enjoyment? (Ecc 2:24–25).

Solomon penned these words following a long list of accomplishments such as amassing gold and silver, great houses, gardens, parks and vineyards, all of which to him were vanity. His conclusion was, a man can do nothing better than to find satisfaction in his work. Not only does satisfaction come as a gift at the hand of God, but it comes through following his precepts and is directly related to the character he is attempting to develop in family members. Our society would tend to associate satisfaction with pleasure but the biblical concept is more involved with integrity.

The secular world can focus on the price they are receiving and more often than not seem to get away with it. However, Christian commitment in this issue demands a focus on the quality of the product or service we are providing. This doesn't mean we have no bargaining power, but focusing on job satisfaction may occasionally mean we will be involved in a less lucrative market. In Great Britain Christian writers, for the most part, earn far less than secular writers. Relationship seminars for Christians are done for about a tenth of the fees one could expect from industry. Choosing job satisfaction over material gain is definitely not limited to Christian work, but the key to real job satisfaction is always a focus on what I am selling rather than the price I am receiving for it.

I can just hear Tevye (of *Fiddler on the Roof*) asking God 'Would it upset some great eternal plan if I were a wealthy man?' Surely, it seems, if there were any justice we would concentrate on a good day's work and receive the appropriate wage. Frequently, our attempts to manufacture a bit of 'justice' for ourselves becomes an obsession with price which automatically replaces our concern for service and proportionately increases the amount of pressure in our lives.

We want the extra money to improve our quality of life but stress reduces the quality of life. When the pressure of job dissatisfaction results in stress, the entire family comes under pressure. As various family members succumb to stress this feeds back to other family members. Not only does this chain reaction reduce the quality of life, it also means that the wage earner now has two potential sources of stress. He or she is under pressure on the job and at home.

It has already been stated that the Bible's view of satisfaction has more to do with integrity than pleasure. The major reason for this is that God's emphasis is on character. He is concerned that sensations such as satisfaction, pleasure or enjoyment be derived from things which build and display right character. It is important to understand this because in attempting to use job satisfaction as a principle we may be tempted to conclude that people should immediately move to the type of employment they would most enjoy. Or that someone involved in a fairly routine job cannot possibly find satisfaction in his work. Neither of these is true. We could fail to find satisfaction in what we might have considered the ideal job or find satisfaction in one considered to be boring. We can explore several factors involved in job satisfaction such as the ethics, influences, attitudes and demands of our job.

Some questions we can ask ourselves are:

1. Do I have positive feelings about my employer/ occupation?
   a. Does it produce a product or service which is a contribution to society, or do I feel somewhat guilty for being involved with it?
   b. Are the business practices up front or am I supporting a crook?
   c. Do normal practices require me to take unauthorised or unethical short-cuts?

Real job satisfaction, for a Christian, is not possible without a clear conscience. Added pressure comes from the feeling that the full weight of responsibility for success rests on our shoulders, because we find it hard to ask God to bless an endeavour which we know does not bless him.

2. Do I have a clear conscience about the way I do my job and my attitude towards it?
   a. Am I doing quality work, and would I want my name associated with it?
   b. Am I doing the right quantity of work, giving my employer or customer value for money?
   c. Have I been creative in finding more efficient ways to do my work?
   d. Am I even attempting to find satisfaction in my work, or am I simply viewing it as a means to a pay packet?
   e. Do I take 'recognised' but unauthorised short-cuts?

Many have found job satisfaction in rather unstimulating work through challenging themselves to greater efficiency.

Pride of workmanship is not limited to the product we produce. It extends to the way we maintain our equipment, work area and even personal appearance, but it begins with personal effort concerning our own attitude.

3. Do I feel positive about the practices of my peers?
    a. Am I working under a collective agreement of production levels which is so inefficient that it results in the customer having to pay far more for the product?
    b. Am I co-operating with time and expense accounting practices which are not completely honest?

In the office of one of our friends it was standard practice to have a half day off per week—other staff members would clock out the one who was off. He knew that he could not participate in this, which didn't make him too popular at first, but he was eventually highly respected. He had a job satisfaction which came through integrity.

4. Do I have positive feelings about the expectations of my position?
    a. Can I satisfy the expectations of my position and still have the time, energy and emotional strength to honour my family priorities?
    b. Will career progression conflict with my moral, ethical or family priorities?

We want to earn more money to enhance our quality of life, but what good is it if we can't get off the merry-go-round long enough to sample the quality?

We must also recognise that no amount of money can buy the quality of life that can be obtained through investing time in our families.

The answers to any of these questions may reveal one or more sources of pressure.

This key dimension of finance actually has its roots in the command to love our neighbour. Concern with the quality of our service is a concern for our neighbour where concern with optimal pricing is not. As with any other teaching on love there must be balance. It can always be reduced to an absurdity, because taken to the extreme conclusion we would be giving everything away. I don't believe this rules out bargaining for fair pay. It may adjust some people's ideas of justice.

The 'pay packet mentality' has replaced pride of workmanship. Technology is advancing in a society whose concern with the development of character is on the decline. Unless the emphasis is shifted, this decade will be known for its technological disasters that could have been avoided by old fashioned concepts such as integrity and pride of workmanship. We have already witnessed jumbo jets crashing due to faulty workmanship on the part of the manufacturer, train disasters due to shoddy workmanship in signal maintenance and a great ecological disaster due to a lack of integrity on the part of a tanker captain.

Regardless of the fact that society seems to be on the horns of a dilemma induced by a character crisis, on the personal level there is hope. God honours people who honour his priorities. We have witnessed career and job changes as well as business arrangements altered to honour God. These have resulted in greater job satisfaction and quality of life.

We even know of some who have experienced significant material gains through seeking job satisfaction on God's terms. One of our businessman friends took a large step of faith to end a partnership with a non-Christian and in two years his business was nearly twice the size of the partnership he had left.

We have seen men forced into early retirement for refusing to co-operate with dishonest practices. Others have disadvantaged their careers by stepping out of the fast lane to promotion in order to have time to invest in their families. Some simply refused to sacrifice family time for advantageous involvement in the company social life. Still others have disadvantaged their career prospects through taking a firm stand against the immoral entertainment of clients. Some definitely paid a material price, but none would look back.

THE CONTROLLING FOCUS

The next step is coming to grips with a basic fact.

Financial stability does not depend so much on the amount of money we earn as the way in which we spend it.

Although we may be working hard towards the big financial breakthrough, most of us have come to the realisation that we have far more control over the way we spend our money than the amount we earn. The size of our wage packet is not totally beyond our control. Many can work overtime, others work faster, harder or sell more, but what will you do to add to that? Many are following a well considered strategy towards promotion and are well on track, filling all the right squares. The fact still remains that the actual selection for promotion is not in our control. There are times when earning more money is as difficult as growing another inch in height.

The highway to success is strewn with unrecognised genius and unrewarded efforts. People who make it their business to answer questions regarding the success or failure of business, to their embarrassment, must admit that there is still a degree of mystery. Anyone who has climbed a career ladder is aware there are more qualified people who don't get promoted than do. The point is we may be ready to advance, and may certainly deserve to advance, but although we have done all the right things advancement still eludes us, and with it the additional income which we also deserve. We don't have nearly the control over the amount we earn as we would like to think we do.

Conversely, we do have a lot more control over the amount we spend than a lot of us would like to admit. We don't like to admit the control is there because for many it seems easier to dream of promotion to solve our problems than simply to live within our means until actual promotion allows us to live higher. The fact is that the stress induced through unnecessary financial pressure could be diverting energy that would better be employed toward advancement.

One very well paid client of ours controlled his finances on the income rather than the expenditure side and had been fairly successful at doing so for years. His particular skill was such that he could do as much extra work at home as he cared to. Knowing he had this option he paid little attention to how he spent his money. Whenever his bills seemed to be getting out of hand he would simply do a bit of extra work and pay them off. However, a large part of the reason that he and his wife had come for counselling was he had very little time for his family or his marriage.

There is a myth that says 'One is much more likely to be promoted if one lives (income wise) as though one had already been promoted.' This is convenient because it gives strategic value to 'keeping up with the Joneses'.

This may also be one of the reasons that the business world calls itself 'the rat race'. Thousands living beyond their means in hopes of being able to afford it, forgetting that when they can afford it they will again have to live beyond what they can afford if they hope to avoid stagnation.

The fact that thousands participate in this myth doesn't make it true. It does, however, have the effect of making even those who aren't trying to impress, feel that they should be able to afford things which in fact they cannot.

'If you can resist buying a BMW when all the world around you has to have one—then you'll be a man, my son.'

The truth is that most of the expensive cars are on HP or are tax write offs by corporations who feel they also must sport this veneer of prosperity. One broker who does millions of pounds worth of commercial insurance estimated that 75–80% of all BMWs fell into that latter category.

Coming down to a much more pedestrian level, the fact that we can get the best handle on our finances through expenditures is unpopular even with those of us far below bona fide yuppy status. The idea that we can stay out of debt, have a savings programme and simply do better financially, requires self-discipline, another very unpopular concept.

Our if-it-feels-good-do-it society is financed on the buy-now-pay-later philosophy. This has had the effect of making us creature comfort addicts. We have been brainwashed into believing that life which is not 'comfortable' is sub-standard. We have such an aversion to a sub-standard life that we are willing to mortgage our future to avoid it. For many, stress is the hidden cost of our wall-to-wall high-tech creature comforts.

Any debt, including a mortgage, produces a certain amount of pressure. We know that although we may be able to skip this and skimp on that, this bill must be payed; and that, however slight, is pressure. A second pressure factor is the fact of repayment reducing our available income. On things such as mortgages this pressure is mini-mised by understanding the payment represents the cost of shelter which would otherwise have to be rented. It is also seen as a form of investment or savings.

Our house was certainly an investment: in three years it has nearly doubled in value. We certainly could not afford to purchase it now, but the fact that rising house prices have dramatically advanced our net worth doesn't make the payments any easier to meet. In fact, mortgage interest rates have grown along with the value of our house making us very glad a mortgage is the only debt we have.

This brings us to the worst pressure dynamic: loss of flexibility. The main biblical reason to stay out of debt is not the Romans 13:8 admonition 'Let no debt remain out-standing, except the continuing debt to love one another.' Of far greater concern is the presumptuous attitude that debt represents.

> Now listen, you who say, 'Today or tomorrow we will go to this or that city, spend a year there, carry on business and make money.' Why, you do not even know what will hap-pen tomorrow. What is your life? You are a mist that appears for a little while and then vanishes (Js 4:13–14).

A credit contract presumes three things. It presumes we will be earning the same amount for the term of the contract. It presumes no further demands on our funds for that time. And it presumes that we will have good use for the item for the length of the contract. None of these things is certain. Going into debt reduces our flexibility, which means it could be doubly dangerous with regards to stress. Our unwise spending practices would not only produce the pressure of debt but also reduce our options in gaining job satisfaction should our working conditions change drastically.

Debt is a problem long before one is in hock for a Porsche. Our figures are based on Great Britain but probably represent a trend which is overtaking most of the western world. According to Elizabeth Cook of The Jubilee Centre in Cambridge, the amount of personal debt in Great Britain, not counting mortgages, averages out to £2,400 per family! Half of the families in the country are debt free, which is good but it also makes the average of the rest £4,800. The average annual income is £12,500, but remember, as with any average income figure, the majority of earnings are below that. She also stated they had convincing evidence of debt causing emotional problems such as feelings of isolation, suicidal tendencies and marital breakdown, and that the National Society for the Prevention of Cruelty to Children cites debt as a stress factor in child abuse.

Sarah had no money left in her housekeeping funds when her daughter broke the heel off of the last pair of shoes she could possibly wear for school. She solved the problem by using her Visa card which was also a credit card. After all her mother had brought all of them up paying the local shoe shop a small amount each week. Sarah bought several things out of a catalogue at a small weekly payment. When Christmas came Ian thought it would be a good idea to open an account in a department store, especially since they were advertising that payments were deferred until February. The total payments were beginning to pinch by February. Then the engine went on the family car, on which they were still making payments. This bill for a new engine meant they were in a deep financial crisis.

Len and Shelley Stamp followed a similar route until the debt was slightly higher than their annual income. The pressure it placed on their marriage brought them to us for counselling about five years ago. They made a goal to get out of debt and did without in order to reach it. Shelley informed me that they were out of debt altogether in February and are planning to celebrate the fact in the Autumn, on Crete. The money they were paying out in monthly payments will more than cover the cost of their holiday. It was a real thrill to be able to pay cash for this well deserved trip months before they were to go. It has been a long hard pull but now all the money that comes in belongs to them with no claims on it.

FINANCIAL ONENESS

Financial stress is induced through a wrong focus on earning money, by attempting to control our finances through income rather than expenditure, which usually leads to debt. But possibly the greatest stress factor in the finances of a married couple has to do with the amount of oneness they have in this area.

This was definitely the greatest stress factor in the marriage of Don and Sharon (the marketing consultants mentioned in chapter one). He found the business image myth a very convenient excuse to cater for the 'consumeritis' with which he was afflicted. She knew this and he knew that she knew it. Consequently he simply would not discuss any purchase with her and justified his unilateral decisions as an act of headship.

Possibly the greatest financial safeguard is practising oneness. It is illogical that a couple would wish to become one in every other area and remain single in this area, but it happens every day.

A couple say 'With all my worldly goods I thee endow,' and then go on to talk about his *and* her *money rather than* their *money.*

Many wives who don't go out to work feel they can't actually buy their husbands a present because they would only be spending his money to buy him a gift.

Both partners should feel equally entitled to and equally responsible for finance, regardless of who earns it.

The fact that one partner is employed in the non-profit sector of the family's responsibilities does not diminish his or her share in the partnership.

To accomplish this, the income of both partners must be thrown into one common pot and stirred vigorously until there is no trace of origin. Special accounts in individual names should be avoided. Occasionally there is a specific legal necessity involving a particular estate requirement, etc. Also couples who are frequently separated due to business travel may find it safer for one of them to have a separate account which they know their partner won't be relying on. However, this should be seen as 'funds available to me which will not interfere with my partner's requirements' and not as 'mine to spend as I please'.

Budgeting must be done together by mutual agreement with both partners honestly assessing expenditures. Naturally there will have to be an agreed amount of pocket money for incidentals and some agreement as to the maximum amount for which it seems reasonable for one partner to obligate without consulting the other.

Couples just starting off with little or no finance will not find this a problem. As their assets build they will have developed the habit of joint ownership. However, this will be seen as a very vulnerable arrangement for those who have more at stake, but then what is marriage if it isn't demonstrating the ultimate trust through extreme vulnerability? Should the financial aspect be any exception?

Couples who discuss and pray together over decisions have two additional safeguards not available to those who don't: God and their partner. It would be a rare person who hasn't had times when they felt their partner's in-put regarding a particular decision would provide nothing but unnecessary complication, but every decision of consequence that isn't shared detracts, at least to some degree, from oneness.

The world is looking for proof that Christianity makes a difference and money is their language. Consequently, this is a major source of effective testimony.

FACTS AND ACTION

PERCEPTIONS/THINKING

It is less often a pressure which harms us than how we see or view that pressure.

People whose thinking about pressures is rational, not exaggerated and basically optimistic, are less vulnerable to pressures.

People who see pressures as a threat are more likely to suffer from stress than those who see them as a challenge.

I worry too much   yes—no
I usually expect the worst   yes—no

If YES to either or both:
1. Whenever you feel anxious or worried try to work out the thinking behind it.
   a. What is the specific pressure?
   b. Is your THINKING about it rational?
                              exaggerated?
                              flawed in any way?
   c. Are there other (less pessimistic) ways of thinking about it?
2. Change your thinking so that it is more rational
                              less exaggerated
                              more realistic
                              less pessimistic
3. Tell yourself (out loud if possible) what your new, correct thinking is.

REMEMBER—it is not a pressure or an event or a circumstance which determines whether you will suffer from stress, but your belief and thinking and attitude about it.

THE CHRISTIAN ATTITUDE TO PRESSURES INCLUDES:

1. Getting them into perspective in the light of a pressure free eternity with God to come.
2. Remembering that since you are surrounded by God's love and protection you have no need to fear any pressures—not even death.
3. Seeing pressures as a reminder to become more dependent on God.

If the Christian is worrying unduly about pressures, to the extent that he is suffering stress, then it is likely that his thinking is wrong and needs to be changed. Anxiety may be a lack of faith in disguise.

11

Headship Or Partnership?

We once spent some time discussing marriage preparation with Bishop John Dennis. We agreed that the subject of family structure was becoming very controversial and he said 'Teaching on headship has a lot in common with the Trinity. You may be satisfied with your own understanding but then find it extremely difficult to communicate that understanding to others.'

Secular society has much more influence on the thinking of Christians regarding family life than most of us realise or some would care to admit. The informal education comes through television which models numerous alternative family structures.

Psychologists and sociologists, the more formal spokesmen of our age, tell us the family is simply a system of relationships which, like a car or a washing machine, either works or doesn't work. When the relationship system fails the malfunction is identified in terms of cause and effect rather than right or wrong behaviour. This is a very technical approach which places no responsibility and imposes no value system.

Many psychologists also tend to reflect the trend in modern thinking, which implies that the very existence of authority is the problem. Even books which reluctantly acknowledge the need for authority, are written as though they were groping for a viable alternative.

It is always good to consider our actions in terms of how

they affect others, but that is not the only criteria. There is still right and wrong which demands responsibility which logically implies authority.

Family structure was given by God to avoid the pressures of uncertainty. Unclear roles and vague expectations set the stage for confusion and conflict. When this role structure is misused, it would seem to engender more pressure than it could possibly prevent. Even so, it is utter folly to refer to the family as the basic unit of society and at the same time imply that it should have no structure. According to one Christian writer 'Marriage and the family is the basic origin and building block of society at large, and social government is only an extension of family government.'[1]

What can be done when the structure of government is failing? The options are to change the structure or find out why it is not working. Once assured that the structure is not actually clashing with itself, the people in the structure must come into focus. They can be educated, motivated, or eradicated. Eradication is not available in the family. We can't sack family members (or divorce them) nor can we take them out and shoot them, much as we would like to at times.

An even greater shock to some will be the fact that the option of changing the structure isn't really open to the family either. God has prescribed his structure and we have no authority to change it. In a day and time when totalitarian governments are having to abdicate in favour of democracy it is understandable that democracy is seen as the opposite of oppression and therefore highly favoured by God.

God is definitely against oppression, but we can find no evidence that he has a bias toward democracy. It is not the be-all-and-end-all for every unit of society. Can you imagine children voting on whether they should eat vegetables, or bed times being set by referendum? At what age can they exercise their democratic right to cross a busy street, own a hunting knife or choose their own television programmes? The answer is: when they are sufficiently responsible. But how is that determined—by referendum? It is not wrong for a family to conduct themselves as democratically as possible, but it is unrealistic to consider the family a democracy.

One may say 'Naturally democracy has its limitations raising children but husbands and wives are adults, shouldn't they function as a democracy?' That is mathematically unrealistic since opinions can only be unanimous or split 50/50. Any time the options are limited to agreement or disagreement democracy can't actually be practised. A real majority rule system can't exist when the only possible majority is 100%.

Since we don't have the option of rejecting the structure or shooting dissidents we will have to see what can be done to make the system work. There is something rather paradoxical about eliminating options. We never feel quite free to throw every last ounce of energy into making a thing work when there is the slightest fear that we might be heading in the wrong direction. However, when we are limited to only one option we are freed to bash away with everything we have.

This limitation leads us to conclude that when stress is induced through the family structure, either it isn't God's structure for family life or the structure is being abused at some point.

It is the abuses and not God's structure which cause heartache. Correcting these abuses is not a matter of technical adjustment; it is a matter of confronting the basic selfishness of those who make up the system.

We are concerned that even democracy is under very real threat from selfishness as the majority focus on their rights and pay little attention to their responsibilities.

Selfishness is the primary cause of family dysfunction. Almost every destructive thing which occurs within family relationships can be directly traced to selfishness. It is difficult to imagine any place where it won't manifest itself or any system of government that is impervious to it. Some would want to place a fair amount of the blame on lack of communication but even the majority of that finds its roots in selfishness or self-preservation.

Without authority there is anarchy, but authority seems to invite abuse and rebellion. The human race can be counted on to abuse authority or to rebel against it with the certainty of death and taxes.

Our fallen nature is the key factor, plus the temptation ever present. Some who have been victorious over smoking or drinking are sometimes defeated by over eating. They can stop the use of tobacco or alcohol, but they cannot do away with food. The way we treat authority like the way we treat food is not a once-and-for-all decision. It is an ongoing battle because neither can be done away with.

No one has any idea why God tasked husbands with the responsibility to establish and maintain direction in the family. It certainly does not imply superiority. The problem with having an earth bound mind is that we read too much into God's thinking. We place people into positions of authority because of past superior performance. God doesn't do that any more than he loves us because we deserve to be loved. Most of the leaders God chose in the Bible did not have very impressive records and would not have been selected by modern day experts.

Even more interesting is the fact that some of them wouldn't have had very impressive records after their stint with God because he gave them the sack. We can't assume that God didn't know what he was letting himself in for, so we must assume that God's purposes can be served even through human failures.

This is important because it demonstrates that we are not trusting the leader, we are trusting God to work through his plan. That is a crucial distinction.

Ephesians 5 is only one of many passages which address the issue of family structure, but it is a key passage because it contains the two principal safeguards where this structure concerns husbands and wives.

Now as the church submits to Christ, so also wives should

submit to their husbands in everything. Husbands, love your wives, just as Christ loved the church and gave himself up for her (Eph 5:24–25).

However, each one of you also must love his wife as he loves himself, and the wife must respect her husband (Eph 5:33).

The first safeguard is: Husbands, love your wives. The second safeguard is: the wife must respect her husband.

I am using the term safeguard rather than responsibility because it is the special quality which hallmarks a godly concept of authority. If both partners exercise the particular safeguard they are responsible for the structure will provide the framework for the oneness that God intended. If even one partner is faithful in exercising his or her responsibility, more often than not it will provide the atmosphere God can use to change the other partner. This will even work in some very difficult circumstances.

Carl was a very unassuming, softly spoken, man of about sixty. It was hard to believe he was very near the top of a major corporation. Nancy seemed much more the part, forceful, assertive and much more outspoken. She never said so in so many words, but it was clear that she thought Carl was a wimp. He wouldn't lead out in the home, and gave only tacit co-operation to anything she was trying to accomplish. He was a one man resistance movement. This bothered her but the thing which drove her up the wall was the fact that everyone loved and admired him. His employees went out of their way to tell her how much they enjoyed working for him.

At home Carl had no deep longing to be in charge. He was in charge at work, but not even the extraordinary amount of respect from colleagues and employees could fill his deep longing for respect from Nancy. This is a common problem when an assertive woman begins to feel her husband is very unasserting: she has difficulty respecting him. They were both in the wrong. He should have taken a more positive interest in his marriage—even if he felt she didn't respect him. But the chain reaction was broken and the pressure relieved when Nancy determined to respect and encourage Carl for who he was and to be less concerned with what she would like him to be.

Pat and Jill Williams, in their book *Rekindled*, tell how she became completely 'burnt out' on their marriage after years of his neglecting her in favour of his career. One day she told him, with a glazed look in her eyes: 'I'll cook your meals and wash your clothes and take care of the kids... I'll stay but I can't promise any emotion. Don't expect any response or any real feeling from me, because I don't have anything left.'

Pat realised he was getting what he deserved, but was determined to do everything possible to win his wife back. The book is a record of his long tough journey to prove to his wife that he really did love her. It took a long time and a lot of effort on his part with no response from her to encourage him along the way. However, the mantle of love that was spread over through his continuous efforts, eventually provided the necessary atmosphere to *rekindle* the marriage relationship.[2]

In God's economy leadership is an act of love to those being led, which may shed some light on why Paul parallels love and respect in this context. Jesus used slightly different terminology to make the same point.

> Jesus called them together and said, 'You know that the rulers of the Gentiles lord it over them, and their high officials exercise authority over them. Not so with you. Instead, whoever wants to become great among you must be your servant and whoever wants to be first must be your slave—just as the Son of Man did not come to be served, but to serve, and to give his life as a ransom for many (Mt 20:25–28).

Notice what he says about exercising authority—'Not so with you.' His focus is on servanthood.

Authority was never given for the benefit of the one in authority but as a tool to serve those under that authority.

Abuses of authority place undue pressure on the family adding to the stress potential. Rather than providing a haven from the pressures of the world it becomes a pressure cooker. Unilateral decision making, failure to carry out agreed decisions, using the family assets selfishly, and controlling others as a way of reducing personal stress are the most common abuses.

Unilateral decisions are probably the most common complaint. Some husbands function as if the marriage ceremony involved a wife abdicating all involvement in the decision making process. Not only is it rude to make decisions which affect someone else without consulting them, it is poor leadership. 'People tend to support those decisions that they helped to create,' as the classic principle states.

Don and Sharon, the marketing consultants mentioned in the last chapter, are an extreme example of unilateral decision making, failure to carry out agreed decisions, and using family assets selfishly. His Porsche, time share in Madeira and his new weekend apartment were all decisions made without consulting Sharon. These decisions not only obligated their funds that he was earning, they obligated their funds that she was earning. On more than one occasion he would purchase an item that they had agreed not to buy because they couldn't afford it.

It is difficult to envisage any type of structure without some sort of authority. Authority, like any other power, can be misused. Perhaps the greatest temptation for a person in authority is to use that position to control others as a way of alleviating the pressure on themselves. This is a way of preventing his or her own stress.

Many people were raised up by controllers and went to work for controllers and therefore have no other example of leadership technique. This type of technique is not only a recipe for disaster, it is a recipe for stress. The reason is that no one can control another human being unless they allow themselves to be controlled. Anyone who believes differently hasn't raised teenagers.

Certainly, teenagers can often provoke this type of abuse. Our sixteen-year-old grand daughter is temporarily living with us which gives me added insight. I felt that it could probably be proved that anyone who enjoys the type of music she does and especially at that volume, has a vitamin deficiency which in turn affects the function of their brain. I had seriously considered banning that cacophony as a potential health hazard. But I realised that it would only have been a means of controlling my own stress.

Another example of using one's position as head of the house to control personal stress is the husband who refuses to allow his wife to have driving lessons. He knows that anyone learning to drive is liable to have at least a few dings in their bodywork, if not worse, and he simply doesn't need the added pressure.

Sometimes the guilty parties don't realise just how selfish their behaviour is and will change when it is brought to their attention. Because of this we have a tendency to attribute the problem to ignorance. Husbands and wives who attempt to control each other or the entire family for their own peace of mind, will usually attempt to change if they can be convinced of their motives, but that doesn't mean that ignorance is at the root of the problem. Ignorance perpetuates the problem, just as with the common cold. No one would claim that the source of the common cold is ignorance, even though it is our ignorance of the exact cause which renders us unable to cure it.

We are all aware that we have an extremely selfish old sin nature living within us. We are also aware that this old nature has some pretty clever ploys to gain control. In most cases the old nature doesn't have to use anything too clever. It simply relies on our short sightedness. We like to be in control and most of us feel uncomfortable when we aren't. As the doctor said in chapter four 'When an individual experiences a lack of control they will develop a proportionate level of stress.' It is easy to understand how 'not being in control' would, for many, be an open door to stress. It implies a lack of trust in the one we believe is in control, and certainly in a loving God who is in control. As pagan as that last statement may sound, it is exactly the thing which draws Christians into a 'look out for number one' mentality. If a person in authority has problems remembering that God is in control and never takes a holiday from his responsibility, how much more precarious must the situation of those under that authority seem?

There is a sense in which headship and submission are stretched entirely out of proportion by people on both sides of the argument. Very few reading this book will be hard core women's libbers who believe that marriage is simply a cultural ploy to exploit women. Neither is there likely to be too many men reading this book who function in their marriage as though it were simply a cultural ploy to exploit women. A few more at each end of the spectrum have problems over the concept, but the majority reading this simply function under the concept without too much concern.

Most couples have found their own 'level' of dealing with headship and submission. Some wives are quite happy for their husbands to make nearly all decisions and to function as the big boss. Most of the women who couldn't live that way are married to men who have no desire to either. My point is that the majority are not arguing over male headship. For most Christians it is fairly hypothetical, because it so seldom becomes an issue. The '51%' is seldom invoked. Headship and submission are an integral part of family structure, but a marriage is more than family structure—it is two people becoming one. *In a good marriage, headship would normally be obscured by partnership*. A Christian marriage shouldn't be characterised by an *obvious* authority structure but by *obvious* co-operation.

Most of the people experiencing problems in this area don't really have trouble with the basic concept, but they do have problems with their partner's interpretation of the concept. Sharon didn't have any problem with biblical submission to her husband. She was concerned about his understanding of headship. Don didn't think too much of Sharon's idea of submission because she was always questioning the way he handled the finances.

Men who treat their wives as resources to earn money, but allow them no say in the spending of it, bring pressure into the marriage. We can all see that. We have used some pretty radical cases throughout because they do provide very clear illustrations, but there are many more couples who are bringing unnecessary pressure into their marriage through much more subtle abuses.

There are many ways in which family structure is abused. Some of them are more difficult to spot than others, but all of them create pressure within the family. It doesn't hurt to examine how effectively we are supporting our family structure.

Answer the following questions as if your partner were going to check your answers.

1. My partner and I are equally involved in all significant decisions.
   Usually   Sometimes   Seldom   Never

2. I communicate fully on all matters concerning the direction of the family.
   Usually   Sometimes   Seldom   Never

3. I approach decisions with the best interest of the family at heart—not my own agenda.
   Usually   Sometimes   Seldom   Never

4. I am fulfilling my biblical role as a marriage partner in a way that places no burden on my partner.
   Usually   Sometimes   Seldom   Never

5. My partner has my complete support.
   Usually   Sometimes   Seldom   Never

6. I am direct in my approach to my partner.
   Usually   Sometimes   Seldom   Never

7. I don't attempt to manipulate my partner.
   Usually   Sometimes   Seldom   Never

8. I establish no family rules or policies with my own self-interest at heart.
   Usually   Sometimes   Seldom   Never

9. I don't think I could be justly accused of using our

assets selfishly.

Usually   Sometimes   Seldom   Never

10. We have total financial oneness.

Usually   Sometimes   Seldom   Never

One of the most common problems is the fact that we 'read one another's mail', that is we are far more concerned with God's message to our partner than we are with what he is saying to us. This results in husbands thinking, 'I'll love her when she starts respecting me as she should,' and wives thinking, 'I'll respect him when he begins loving me as he should.' In so doing we have turned God's two safeguards against stress into a 'Catch 22' which actually promotes stress.

The way out of this dilemma is, of course, to assume our responsibilities in the marriage and leave our partner's as a matter between them and God.

God doesn't lay these principles down on the basis of husband love your wife—wife respect your husband because they deserve it, but rather because they need it. God deals with us in love and grace, not because we've earned or deserved it but because of our need. Our attitude towards our partner should be the same—loving and respecting on their bad days as well as their good.

Doing this requires understanding that this concept comes from a loving God, who has a plan and goal for our life. We need the assurance that he never takes a holiday from his responsibilities, and the awareness that he is holding us responsible for the way we function in our marriage. In other words it is a classical application for all four of the Basic Basics of chapter four.

NOTES

1. 'Civil Disobedience' by Jeremy Jackson in *Life and Light*, Autumn 1987 pp 6–7 (Greater Syracuse Christian Action Council).
2. Pat and Jill Williams *Rekindled* Fleming Revell Co, page 23.

FACTS AND ACTION

OBJECTIVES IN LIFE

Think about and write down your objective for:

> your work
> your spouse
> your children
> your neighbours
> your finances
> yourself
> your church

Can I control these objectives?   yes—no

Are these objectives correct and wise?   yes—no

If NO—what do you intend to do about them?

REMEMBER—the only controllable objectives are:

> —to do your best
> —to do what is right

Christian teaching goes further.

1. Your overriding objective should be, in all things, to please God
2. Prayer changes things

I believe that prayer changes things   yes—no

If YES—do you pray about people and things you have no control over, to bring about legitimate and good desires?

12

Stress In The Bedroom

We begin our seminars on marriage preparation by saying there are three major sources of marriage problems:

Men and women are different
They are both sinners
They are influenced by the philosophy of the age.

Everyone laughs when we cite differences between men and women as a cause of marital problems. With some it is a laugh one gives when a human idiosyncrasy has been underscored in a play. It says 'You've hit the nail on the head.' Others simply think we are making a joke. We doubt that very many have a real idea of the extent to which that statement applies. Certainly our understanding of the impact of these differences continues to grow with our experience in this field.

A few years ago one might have been able to insert a little chuckle here, pointing out that this 'problem area' of men and women being different is the very thing which makes sexual relations possible. Unfortunately that would be challenged today.

As men and women we differ in the most minute particles of our being: there is a chromosome combination which has stamped our gender on each cell in our body. The dozens of other physically measurable differences are only the tip of the iceberg. Rob Parsons, director of Care

STRESS IN THE BEDROOM 171

for the Family, announced to his family that he was going to be spending a few hours in his study to write an article on the difference between men and women. One of his children asked if it would help if he drew him a picture. The problem is that many of us don't expand our understanding very far beyond this in our adult life. We err greatly if we think that the main gender difference is a matter of 'plumbing' or that women are simply 'lumpy men'.

There is a lot of evidence to conclude that the same hormones which are responsible for the physical differences also masculinise or feminise the brain. The fact that men and women have such differing thought processes is a far greater obstacle to fulfilling sexual relations than physical problems, on a ratio of about 100 to one.

There are several reasons for this last statement. One is that this variation affects every area of our relationship, and sexual relations are a celebration of that relationship. Consequently, if our different perspectives cause a falling out over decorating the lounge, and we don't get it settled, it affects our relationship and we may rightly expect it to have repercussions in our love life.

A second reason is the vast majority of sexual problems are problems in our thinking. Sexual relations are not simply physical. The two not only become one flesh they also become one in soul and spirit, which is far more significant than mere copulation. It has been said that our brain is our most important sex organ. Naturally male/female perspectives must be respected if not blended. It is our personal experience, after thirty-eight years of marriage, that many of these male/female differences in sexual expectations can actually blend. That is not a very scientific sampling on which to make such a statement, but it makes sense that two people committed to pleasing each other will blend in a lot of areas.

We think the main cause of pressure in this area of differences has to do with a particular mystique regarding sex which may have played a part in the civilising of the human race.

There is, in our opinion, a very valid stereotype regarding the fact that women have always done a better job of maintaining the balance between the physical act of sex and relationship commitment. This stereotype is illustrated in the song 'Love and Marriage' which says: 'Dad was told by Mother, "You can't have one without the other." '

Man has been stereotyped down through the ages as the barbarian who is domesticated by the more civilised female dragging him kicking and screaming into family life. Sex and commitment, as a generality, have far less relationship to a man. Sexual relations to a man seem to be as external as his genitalia, while to women they are a much more integral part of her being. On a similar note Lord Byron said 'Man's love to man's life is a thing apart, tis woman's whole existence.'

Could it be that this feminine outlook on sex has played a key role in the civilisation of the human race? By the same token is the women's lib movement a statement that women are getting tired of their role as civilisers and want their turn at being the barbarians?

Please keep in mind that these are generalities and for every generality there are several exceptions. However, the value of examining any time honoured generalities is that we learn to be more sensitive to our partners. Not that our partner will always fit the mould but it does provide a starting point.

One positive result of understanding this mystique is it helps men to understand why women are so slow to respond to love making.

The fact that there is such a strong link between the relationship and making love means that a woman must be approached through the relationship, rather than through her body.

Frequently the best aphrodisiac is an intimate conversation, and it could even have more emphasis on the conversation than the intimate. Even when she is wanting physical contact it is not necessarily in a way which makes sense to a man. After all shoulders, arms and the outer aspects of the thigh are not exactly erogenous zones to a man.

With men the psychological has almost instant access to

the biological—a thought can cause an erection. I hasten to say this diminishes with age; many middle-aged wives wish their husbands still had that problem. What men seem never to lose is their unifocal perspective. While some women are one big erogenous zone from their finger tips to their toe nails, their husband's sensitivity is focused on a limited area around his penis.

There is a contrast between a fairly narrow band of physical sensitivity in men to a very broad band of physical sensitivity in women. I would suggest that there is a connection between this and the psychological mystique discussed earlier. The broad feminine perspective views sex in the context of love and commitment, contrasted with the narrow male perspective of sex for the sake of sex. The important thing is there is a difference and marriage partners who underrate this are inviting frustration into their marriage bed.

This brings up another idiosyncrasy which causes problems; the words bed and sex are far too closely related. Most sexual relations occur in bed. A nice clean comfortable bed has an important role to play in love making but it's the timing we are concerned about.

All too often the first signal of amorous intentions occurs after the light has been turned out for the night. That is light-years too late!

This, we believe, is to some extent because there is such strong association between sex and bed. Men think about making love, but realise that this won't take place until they retire for the night, and so the time to make those intentions known is in bed.

Love making begins at breakfast! Any experience which begins as the result of two bodies sharing the same bed, or last minute invitations, is not worthy to be called love making. It is not *of the relationship*, it is strictly chemistry and while it may be enjoyable to both this source of enjoyment is too chancy to be risked with any frequency. At best it should be considered a youthful idiosyncrasy.

Both partners need to be aware of the need to take this part of their relationship very seriously. Song writers write of chemistry, but sadly few of them have ever done any marriage counselling. This might be excusable if chemistry was something which only eluded the middle-aged, but the fact is as many as 50% of marriages are not consummated on the wedding night because couples are relying too heavily upon chemistry. Again let us stress that the brain is our most important sex organ. This, coupled with the knowledge that there are many other factors such as physical stamina and the everyday concerns of life, means that lovemaking requires some advance consideration, if not actual scheduling.

The fact that a marriage consists of two sinners means that we easily fall for the world's philosophy of sex, which is 'I have needs and I have a right to have my needs met.' This focus, which is 180 degrees out of phase with Christianity, is probably the greatest single source of pressure in our love life.

This manifests itself in several ways. Sometimes it is very overt selfishness such as the case mentioned in chapter one. 'We have sex every night. My husband won't take no even when I am unwell. I say sex not love making for that is what it has become, just the same old act. I do love him and would value some helpful instruction.'

We occasionally hear of middle-aged men who 'require' sexual relations every night. There would be nothing wrong with this if their partner ran on the same schedule, but I doubt that is ever the case. One thing this nightly schedule reveals is a lack of romantic atmosphere. We find it difficult to believe that a middle-aged couple can do justice to the act of marriage on a nightly basis. If they can it is because they have very few responsibilities to clutter their minds. We wonder how frequently the wife reaches an orgasm. We heard of one middle-aged woman who didn't enjoy sex but looked forward to it because it was the only time she ever had her husband on her own. Such men are not making love to their wives, they are simply copulating!

It is also a purely selfish focus which only considers our partner's needs as a matter of technique rather than out of genuine concern. This regards them as an instrument to be played rather than a living vessel into which we pour all our love as partners in a loving experience.

If you want to induce real pressure in the marriage, try violating several principles at once. Because we constantly run an advert for Mission to Marriage, we receive a lot of anonymous phone calls from people who are desperate. One wife of an evangelical church leader shared how her husband had no concept of making love. Firstly, he demanded intercourse on the basis of 1 Corinthians 7 (which is a perversion of the passage). Secondly, as head of the house he set the scenario, and thirdly, when she would make any attempt at foreplay he would grumble something to the effect that she should 'hurry up and get along with it'. It's guys like that I would love to counsel—with a horse whip.

An additional pressure introduced through this selfish focus comes from the fact that selfishness is hard to please. If my pleasure comes mainly from the sensations of sex, my personal gratification will very likely diminish and I will be looking for more exotic practices and techniques to boost my faltering level of pleasure. This often places pressure on the partner to enter into practices with which they are not comfortable, and may lead to other partners. One couple we counselled had actually gone so far as to fantasise jointly that there was a third person in bed with them while they were making love.

The Bible makes husbands and wives responsible to meet their partner's needs. 1 Corinthians 7 talks about husbands and wives having a duty toward their partner. This duty was clearly not simply to allow their partner to use their body toward procreation, because Paul states they should not abstain from these relations except for periods of fasting so that they would not be tempted. He was obviously discussing pleasure. It is equally obvious that is a relationship which is entered into with the individual's concern focused on their partner's needs. This is possible when they know that their partner is totally occupied with their pleasure. Even if our partner is not as sensitive as they might be, having the right focus makes sexual relations much more fulfilling than when our main concern is ourselves.

The principle of sacrificial love mentioned in chapter five which stated 'The paradox of life is that happiness cannot be attained by directly seeking it,' is just as valid in our sexual relations. We have received criticism that this is a naive approach to sexual relations. Certainly our own desires play a significant role in sexual relations because without them our partner would have nothing to fulfil.

Naturally we must communicate those desires to our partner and also give some feedback as to the accuracy of their efforts. But that doesn't detract from the basic proposition that we focus on our partner's needs and leave them to concentrate on ours.

1 Corinthians 10:24 clearly says, 'Nobody should seek his own good, but the good of others.' (Regarding this topic we limit the number of others to one.) Committing ourselves to greater concern with our partner's needs than our own is a rather vulnerable proposition. However if I can't trust God to work through his principles with a partner who loves me, could I possibly put this into practice out in the world?

We have not yet mentioned the most blatant form of placing our needs over the needs of our partner—adultery. This is also one of the greatest pressures that can be brought into a relationship. This is no stranger to the church. It would be less of a problem for Christians if it were a simple matter of physical cravings and lust.

The adversary is out to break up Christian marriages and he is more subtle than to try tempting us through the usual sensual approaches. Many an affair has actually begun through a spiritual attraction. Alice shared something in the house group and John was the only one who actually seemed to understand and empathised with her. They shared a bit further during coffee and he demonstrated real mature insight. It also seemed they were both on the same spiritual wavelength—how refreshing.

Two weeks later when John's wife couldn't understand the spiritual implications of a decision that faced them he headed straight for Alice, assuming she could give him a feminine perspective on the problem. She didn't disappoint him; she provided exactly the insight he needed. From that point there was scarcely a meeting during which they failed to find some opportunity to share. The problem was greatly intensified when Alice was elected to the Parish Council of which John was already a member. This made legitimate opportunities to meet in each other's homes on church business.

We have seen this scenario several times. Two really committed Christians in an affair that began with the most innocent of motives. An affair was the last thing on their minds. Possibly it not being on their minds explains why they were not alert. We need to be more aware of just how vulnerable we are. There is a danger any time we are attracted to a person of the opposite sex, even when that attraction has nothing to do with the physical.

God meant for us to become one and enjoy intimacy in every area with our partner. Through a lack of understanding or time pressure we may find someone else meeting our emotional or spiritual longings to be real or feel close. Suddenly we find ourselves thinking of this person more and finding excuses to talk to them. Our sharing may then become deeper and we find them meeting needs our partner is not. It is at this point the fantasy begins: 'What would it be like being married to this person?' We need to get control of our thoughts and turn them back to our spouse. God will help us to establish that same meaningful spiritual or psychological oneness with our marriage partner. It may take a lot of time and effort but God is on our side and wants to bring us into oneness.

The primary control is in our thought life. This is not limited to problems of faithfulness; the entire battle against stress is a battle of the mind. Before we can make any meaningful progress in this direction we must distinguish between subjective and objective thinking.

Subjective thinking centres around me and the way I feel regarding various issues. It ranges from desire for a particular thing, to fear that we will be deprived of something near

and dear to us. People who are said to be 'controlled by
their emotions' are mainly subjective thinkers. Not all subjectivity is bad. Zeal, fervour and enthusiasm are subjective, but so are greed, lust and bitterness. It is usually our
subjective thinking that gets us into trouble.

Objective thinking is free of personal feelings or preju-
dice and totally unbiased. Objectivity examines only the
facts and does not reach opinions based on feelings or
desires. Objectivity approaches the situation, inventorys
the possibilities and forms a plan. Objective thinkers are
often accused of having no feeling or heart. The contrast is
sometimes made between thinking with our heart or our
mind; the heart being subjective. Christians sometimes act
as if all valid spiritual thinking is 'with the heart', forgetting
we are told to love the Lord 'with all our heart, soul and
mind'. We hasten to add that it is not an either-or situation.
Both subjectivity and objectivity have their place. The
thing to remember is no amount of subjective thinking will
ever get us out of a rut in our thinking.

Ephesians 4:20–29 speaks of the process of change in
terms of very specific decisions to *put off and put on*.
Dealing with sinful thought patterns involves a definite
decision to change thought patterns, not simply to stop the
wrong thinking, but to replace it with right thinking. This
begins with a decision to put off subjective thinking on this
matter and to replace it with objective thinking.

We must discipline ourselves to move into an objective
grasp of the facts. For instance, 'My wife doesn't meet a
particular need that this woman does.' The truth is no
woman is perfect and there will always be other women
who are better than she in a particular area, but how many
other needs does your partner meet? I frequently meet
women whom, for one reason or another, I find quite
attractive, but there are very few who don't sooner or later
make me really appreciate the one I have. Even of those
few who stand the test of time, reason tells me that were I
married to them I would discover a lot more flaws. 'The
grass is greener' syndrome can be stood on its head by

examining the facts and redirecting our focus to those positive qualities our partner does have.

There are several precautions against developing relationships with a dangerous potential which are extremely reasonable.

As much as possible attend meetings as a couple and function as a couple. This is a statement to yourself, your partner and the world that you are one of a pair. We hesitate to put this in because it can be over done: occasionally couples almost smother each other. And we recognise that husbands and wives are whole and complete individuals who need their own space. However, we are saying this, even at the risk of being misinterpreted, because of the far larger group of marriage partners who function as 'married singles'. We are talking of people who hardly go out together and when they finally do, they are hardly ever seen together.

Try never to share with someone of the opposite sex those inner feelings you haven't already shared with your spouse. Some have gone so far as to label this verbal adultery.

Challenge yourself as to the appropriateness or necessity of time alone with a person of the opposite sex.

Ask yourself a few questions:

> Am I attracted to this person spiritually, psychologically or physically?
> Does this person seem to understand or appreciate me more than my partner?
> Is my relationship with my partner under pressure now for any reason?
> Is it boring?

Finally, make a commitment never to think romantically about anyone other than your partner. All adultery begins with wrong thinking and it can be nipped in the bud with such a commitment.

Let me summarise these main pressure points regarding sexual relations.

Men and women are different. These differences must be recognised, respected, explored and the understanding gained made part of our approach to each other in lovemaking.

We are basically selfish. This most commonly manifests itself in failure to respect the above differences, but occasionally it blatantly ignores the needs of the partner altogether.

The philosophy of the age has influenced us. This is the Hedonistic notion that we have the right to have our sexual needs met rather than a responsibility to meet our partner's needs. It is a quite natural outgrowth of the fact that we are basically selfish.

The mind is the most crucial element in romance, which is why this chapter links love life with thought life. It is effective stewardship of our thought processes which will keep us from adultery. Good mental stewardship will give us sensitivity in meeting the desires of our partner. An alert mind will also guard against the philosophy of the age reversing the values concerning God's gift of sex.

A SUMMARY QUESTIONNAIRE

This questionnaire will indicate how vulnerable to pressure you are.

1 = very strongly disagree   4 = agree
2 = strongly disagree   5 = strongly agree
3 = disagree   6 = very strongly agree

1   I have many pressures in my life   1 2 3 4 5 6

2   I am a Type A   1 2 3 4 5 6

3   I am unemotional   1 2 3 4 5 6

4   I often bear resentment   1 2 3 4 5 6

5   I often feel hopeless and helpless   1 2 3 4 5 6

6   I get good support   1 2 3 4 5 6

7   I keep physically fit (as far as exercise,   1 2 3 4 5 6
     weight, diet, smoking, and alcohol are
     concerned)

8 I have a healthy life style as far as rest,   1 2 3 4 5 6
   relaxation, delegation, use of time,
   meditation and sharing problems are
   concerned

9 My priorities are correct   1 2 3 4 5 6

10 I have a good self-image   1 2 3 4 5 6

11 My thinking is 'good'   1 2 3 4 5 6

12 I get my love, security and significance from   1 2 3 4 5 6
   completely reliable sources

13 My overall objective is to do my best rather   1 2 3 4 5 6
   than 'win'

14 My overall objective is to please God   1 2 3 4 5 6

15 I believe that everything has a purpose for   1 2 3 4 5 6
   my good

16 I thank God for everything   1 2 3 4 5 6

High scores in questions 1–5 and low scores in 6–16 could mean you are vulnerable to stressors and at risk of suffering stress.

Summary

The Purpose of Pressure

Marriage is probably the greatest arena of human conflict known to mankind. Many experience it as a crucible for refining human character. It can also be the greatest source of human comfort and encouragement, but too few experience that. Marriages don't, in a technical sense, produce stress. They can, however, produce tension and pressure, which are contributing factors. God's wisdom shows us how we can live in such a way as to minimise pressure within the home and allow the intended comfort and encouragement to blossom. The home is then a sanctuary for family members to find refuge from the pressures of the world; it becomes a support system.

Christians are not immune to the pressures of life. In fact, Jesus promised us that in this world we would have trouble, which could also have been translated pressure. Biblical priorities can help us avoid some, but many are unavoidable. Christians are not immune to stress either, but we are much better equipped to prevent it. If this were not so the gospel of peace would have very little to speak into this generation. Pressure is the hallmark of our times, because for many, life is lived in the fast lane.

There is a temptation to say, 'We just need to slow down.' That could be as naive as telling the mother of three preschoolers that she needs to rest. It presumes greed and status are the only things which keep people in the fast lane. The fact is, it is not always possible to slow down appreciably. In some instances it would amount to little less than a retreat from life. Many occupations only run in the fast lane and there are few if any positions of responsibility in large corporations that don't entail a fair amount of pressure. If there is to be a Christian presence in critical and influential places in society then some Christians will have to live in the fast lane. If God has called us into the fast lane, he has a survival plan as well.

We hasten to clarify, there are times when company policy will not allow a person to honour his or her God given priorities which may be a signal for that person to move out of the fast lane.

The philosophy of the age is changing the face of western culture, and it unfortunately has enormous influence on Christian behaviour. On the one hand, it raises pseudo intellectual arguments denying human responsibility, and on the other, it normalises sin. Divorce and fornication have become social norms with adultery gradually gaining the same acceptance. However, the major distinction between the philosophy of the age and a Christian world view is much more basic. It is the watershed issue of whether selfishness is a right or a problem.

In a society which claims there is no such thing as right and wrong, selfishness cannot be condemned. Therefore, it is not a problem, it is a right. However, God has condemned selfishness in no uncertain terms, calling us at the same time to a quality of love that is the antithesis of selfishness. Unfortunately, secular thinking has considerable influence over Christians for two main reasons: 1. We find their rationale convenient, 2. Many of us have lost sight of the character and credibility of the Creator. This has caused a crisis of faith leaving us unsure as to whether we can survive in today's world without at least bending a few of God's commandments.

Human responsibility has been jettisoned for fear of provoking guilt, because we have lost sight of the fact that God is the author of true moral guilt. It is God's 'wheel clamp', a tool to drive us to the only One in the universe who can permanently remove it. The statement 'God is love' to many means he overlooks our short comings. We have failed to see 'God is love' in the light of God's overarching goal to develop the character of Christ in our lives. We also quite easily lose sight of the fact that the sovereignty of God speaks of his ability to orchestrate events in our lives to reach this objective. Failure to comprehend this plays a major role in most marital difficulties. We forget God is in control even when life is difficult. We may lack this awareness because we have never consciously offered God the control of our life. We may have committed various issues or problems to him, but never really thought about committing the whole of our life to him.

Our spiritual life began when the Lord Jesus accepted us where we were. He made no demands that we achieve a certain level of holiness before he would receive us. We had only to admit our destitute condition and accept his grace. However, if a king were going to adopt a pauper into his family he would also be kind enough to make provision for the pauper to shed his impoverished identity and acquire everything necessary to be comfortable in his new family.

The Christian life is more than acceptance into the royal family and more than wearing royal robes. It goes far deeper than external appearances.

God intends us to develop the royal character which will flow from within. Christianity is more than arriving at the palace door. It is an ongoing journey to develop the character of the King. This journey is not conducted in the luxury of the palace. It is walking through hard places in the world. We haven't been thrown, as it were, to the lions. We have the King's royal presence in the form of his Spirit, plus his own authorised guide book which promises to have all the information necessary for the journey. It reminds me of the rugged 'Outward Bound' frontier camping trips that major companies send their executives on to develop certain qualities in them.

Christianity is a way of life—not following principles discovered by man but those laid down by the Author of life. Because of this we know it is pure truth and therefore the most effective system for living possible. However, to believe a system is all we need for life is as arrogant as ignoring it is under responsible. It is a little like assuming that being a famous chef consists of no more than owning a good collection of recipes.

Christianity is a relationship with the King. It consists of more than a 'snuggle up in Father's lap' type of relationship, as nice as that is. This relationship provides the power to hold on course throughout the journey. Preoccupation with the snug aspect of the relationship is to lose sight of the Father's objective and thereby run the risk of a rather grotesque perpetual childhood.

The Christian life is more than following a code of ethics. What it means to live the life and what it means to rely on the relationship are brought into perspective only when we fully understand the goal of being conformed to the image of Christ. Following the guide book with this goal in mind is much more than 'successful living'; it is growing more like the Father through learning to please the Father.

The goal of building a Christ-like character requires more than a snug relationship; it also requires an intimate, soul searching, sometimes painful relationship with him. Because I do not have the character of Christ, and that is the goal of a Christian life, I must change. Because I will not completely attain that goal in this life I must be continually changing. Because the process of change is seldom comfortable I must face the prospect that my life will not be filled with comfort—a thing that I long for.

Does it sound bleak, talking of a life that will never be really comfortable, because there will always be a certain amount of pressure? Then remember the pressure is to produce growth.

Handle pressure God's way and develop maturity. Mishandle it and develop stress.

Stress is not from the pressures of life; it is my reaction to the pressures of life. In most instances stress is a self-inflicted wound.

All Scripture is God-breathed and is useful for teaching, rebuking, correcting, and training in righteousness, so that the man of God may be thoroughly equipped for every good work (2 Tim 3:16–17).

It is the rebuking part I am interested in here. When I am not growing I find the Bible constantly rebuking me. Not only while actually reading it, but in every day situations as I make inappropriate responses to life, the word comes back to me.

The next word after rebuking is 'correcting'. The word doesn't come back to haunt me; it comes to encourage me to correct my course and it provides for that correction. Often this involves such old fashioned concepts as 'confession' and 'repentance'. A good deal of the stress in a marriage relationship is caused by violating the very simple but basic principle found at the end of Romans 12: 'Overcome evil with good.' Our natural response is to 'return evil for evil'.

I made a mistake recently and as I discussed it with Joyce, she responded in a sharpish tone of voice, so I snapped back at her something about a guilt trip. Unfortunately something interrupted us before it was put right. In times past I might have allowed that to pass in the hopes it would be forgotten, but not any more. Harsh words to one's spouse are not pleasing to God any more than they are pleasing to the offended partner, and I want to demonstrate love to both. Ignoring that I have been rude doesn't bless either one of us. It's dishonest, and from a purely relational perspective, it creates tension between us. I can't think of many things more misleading than the often quoted: 'Love is never having to say sorry.'

A few harsh words may sound like 'small potatoes', or like I'm making a mountain out of a mole hill, but it is the way we respond to such situations which controls the stress level in our marriage. One of the most devastating things in a marriage is continually to sweep things like this under the carpet. Another is very closely related—failure to address problem issues because we know it will be uncomfortable. This 'saving trouble for another day' causes resentment which distorts our ability to evaluate accurately the daily transactions in our relationship, usually making things seem far worse than they are. It also lays the ground work for a really good blow up.

Failure to deal with such issues is saying 'I am more concerned with my own immediate comfort than the long range good of our relationship.' This type of selfishness is also at the root of our failure to engage in real open, honest communication. Being a self-disclosing individual is a form of giving which has a price tag. It costs a certain amount of security each time we make ourselves that vulnerable. Failure to give in this way is to demand a relationship on our terms.

Most husbands would be disappointed if their wives wanted a marriage without sex, but millions of husbands want a marriage without deep, open communication.

They want the physical aspect to be deep but the rest kept shallow. This is a lopsided relationship indeed because it limits oneness to the physical. Communication is the fuel of relationship and the agent of oneness. Love requires vulnerability—being vulnerable enough to share weaknesses or to confront our partner over problem issues.

The factor in any relationship with the greatest potential for producing stress is resentment. Failure to forgive produces resentment which not only poisons the relationship, it actually poisons our own bodies. No other stress producing dynamic falls so clearly into the category of a self-inflicted wound than failure to forgive. Life is not ruined by the sins committed against us but by the way we respond to them. We don't develop stress as a result of someone else's sin; it is a result of our own. God makes forgiveness mandatory. When we violate this command we make ourselves and all around us miserable.

We have control of the main stress factor in our lives. It is our response to each other.

There is a sense in which none of us is ready to have a life partner until we don't need one. We shouldn't marry because we need another person just to make it through life. However, many of us, to one degree or another, do just that. We marry, looking to our partner to fulfil basic crucial longings which can only be satisfactorily met by God. This unrealistic requirement places pressure on our partner and on our marriage. We have a crucial longing for love and significance. Love and significance are the exact things which naturally accrue as a result of our relationship with Christ. Without this sense of being loved and significant our sense of personal worth is very low. This brings self-sensitivity, defensiveness and competition, all of which contribute to stress in both partners.

The way out of this is not through finding ways to feel good about ourselves. Finding places where we can excel or people who build us up are very precarious answers. We can accept our personal worth as a part of our heritage in Christ or compete for it on the world's standards, but true human worth cannot be found apart from God.

The most secure road to a healthy self-image is the road which leads to maturity in Christ.

It may sound as if we are offering the goal of Romans 8:29 (being conformed to the image of Christ) as a panacea to all life's problems, that's not so. The road to maturity in Christ is not a smooth one, but there is a definite sense in which things function more effectively when used according to their original design. I can remember teaching a course in conjunction with a Billy Graham crusade. We were using a series of diagrams to depict the condition of the human race. The first was a perfect circle—man in his unfallen state. Next came the fall, a shape that one would not associate with a circle without the first illustration. It had several arrows pressing in depicting the influences of sin, each distorting the original shape. The final illustration had a cross in the centre with arrows exerting pressure against the outside forces. This was to depict the Holy Spirit in the life of the believer untwisting that which was twisted at the fall.

A commitment to maturity in Christ is a commitment to cooperation with God to untwist that which is twisted.

The nearer we come to the original design the more effectively we will function, even in this fallen society. Life never becomes easy, but the storms are far easier to weather in the knowledge that we are under the protection of a loving God who is sovereign over the forces of life. This is especially true when we know that he is allowing nothing to enter our life without a purpose. And for no sound theological reason I feel much more confident going through the trials of life if I know I have been making it my business to please him.

One final issue, we have refered to stress using the analogy of a 'self-inflicted wound' which implies we have 'shot our self in the foot' any time we are stressed. Does this mean that stress is sinful? After all we have said that stress results from an inappropriate response to life pressures. If the right response is God's way, a wrong response must be sin. There is definitely scope for those with a very black-and-white mentality to formulate a very rigid position. However, there are several things to consider before we accuse every one with ulcers of backsliding. First off, stress related ulcers are only a physical manifestation of our psychological response and therefore only a symptom. As with all symptoms it doesn't tell the whole story.

A pastor friend of ours was diagnosed as having ulcers. He was open with his congregation about it. His honesty was rewarded with a long line of Job's counsellors wanting him to 'turn things over to God'. This might well have been the case, his congregation had been very unsupportive at the time. However, a single symptom is never a complete diagnosis. One can have a stomach ulcer without any related stress. Even when an ulcer is stress related it is no measure of spirituality, for the simple reason a certain amount of physical frailty must exist in any organ for it to become a victim of stress. Excess stress will manifest itself at the weakest point. His stomach was evidently substandard which doesn't exactly detract from his spirituality, any more than a cast iron belly makes one a spiritual giant.

Ah, say the black & white-ists, you admit he may have had a little bit of stress, doesn't that imply a little bit of sin? Possibly. Even the most saintly, on occasion find their initial response to certain situations is stressful. They find themselves angry and wrestling with their emotions trying to get their attitudes under control and above all not to say or do anything that will be hurtful. I feel that way frequently, but unfortunately I'm not always successful at saying the right thing. At any rate, these wrestling matches with one's attitudes are not without stress.

Is it possible to be in a wrestling match with ones attitude without being in sin? Paul seems to think one can be angry without sinning. In Ephesians 4:26 he says 'in your anger do not sin', which means to us that we should be wrestling to be sure we don't just blast off at others.

I have found myself at odds with others over a particular policy or procedure and on occasions while arguing my case I began to feel my stomach knot up. To me this was an alarm, a signal that the situation was getting out of hand and I couldn't blame my knotted up stomach on any one but me. I needed to slow down the fervour of my attack or defence, back off and see what tricks my mind was playing on me. Generally, I find in these situations that I am believing the worst about the other person and his or her ideas. It should also be obvious that my lack of stomach ulcers does not attest to my holiness, it is much more likely that I have a tough stomach.

We don't believe finding ourselves in a state of stress is necessarily a sin.

We see stress as the flashing red light on the instrument panel warning us when we aren't handling things correctly. The problem is not in experiencing stress, it is accepting stress as inevitable.

There is an old saying regarding sinful thoughts which goes; 'You are not responsible if a bird lands on your head, but you don't have to let him build a nest there'. In other words the fact that a lustful thought may come into our mind doesn't necessarily constitute sin, but developing, encouraging and enjoying it definitely does.

God has compassion and understanding when we are stressed, he wants to comfort us. However, he wants to do something much more loving than to help us merely to cope with stress, he wants to help us resolve it and prevent it. I repeat; pressure is to produce growth. If we handle pressure God's way we develop maturity, if we mishandle it we develop stress.

FACTS AND ACTION

WHERE ARE YOU ON THE PRESSURE/PERFORMANCE GRAPH?

As pressures increase so does performance—up to a point.

PERFORMANCE

PRESSURES

a = no pressure and no performance = dead
b = not enough pressure = boredom
c = enough pressure to bring out the best performance
d = too much pressure = fatigue—exhaustion
e = even more pressure = ill health
f = breakdown performance

Plot where you are now and where you would like to be

YOU CAN BE IN THE (c) AREA MOST OF THE TIME—BY APPROPRIATING GOD'S PLAN FOR EFFECTIVE LIVING.